The Time For Justice

How the excesses of time have broken our civil justice system

Anthony V. Curto

with Ronald E. Roel

ISBN: 978-0-9849005-1-0

Published by Onward Publishing Inc. Northport, NY 11768

Jacket design and illustration by
Bruce McGowin and Anthony Stiso

First Edition

This book is dedicated to
Linda, Karen, Andrew and Ilse,
all of whom I love.

TABLE OF CONTENTS

Prologue

"Justice delayed is justice denied."
—Former British Prime Minister William Gladstone, from an 1868 speech on Irish self-rule

It was the spring of 1960—my last semester of law school in New York City. I was an impatient student, ready to charge into the real-life practice of law. (I completed my degree in two years instead of the usual three.)

Like many idealistic young lawyers, I felt a sense of urgency, inspired by the classic cases of American jurisprudence. Yet I found myself irresistibly drawn to another, more prosaic case—one appearing every day on the front pages of the city's newspapers.

At the center of this civil lawsuit was Adam Clayton Powell, Jr., a powerful and flamboyant congressman and clergyman from Harlem who was accused of defaming one of his constituents, Esther James. While Powell, the first black representative from New York, was certainly a controversial figure—he built an impressive roster of both friends and enemies over the years—the key legal issue was rather ordinary. Did Powell defame this woman? What was the court's decision? And how was it implemented?

Powell was found liable and ordered to pay damages. A verdict followed by a judgment; that should have been pretty automatic, right?

Not so. As the case unfolded over the next several years, I began to see the imperfections in our legal system—how easily its weaknesses could be manipulated for personal gain and avoidance of responsibility. With each meandering turn in the legal highway paved by *James v. Powell*, I became more and more fascinated. I saw it as a test of the whole legal system—a system that was designed to bring about justice, but ultimately failed. Although the case eventually achieved some modest results, they were obfuscated by a plethora of procedural missteps. Even the plaintiff, flummoxed in her efforts to collect the judgment, ended up abusing the courts with procedural mayhem.

In the end, Powell and his pursuers were mere players in the legal contest; it was the system itself that was put down.

Today, after practicing law for almost 50 years, I am still profoundly influenced by the Powell case. True, the case remains largely a footnote in legal history. Powell's long legacy in Congress has been replaced by an even longer one, that of Charles Rangel, who has occupied his seat for more than 19 terms. Even the monetary judgments involved in the Powell case seem modest by today's standards.

Yet the lessons delivered by *James v. Powell* remain fresh and remarkably relevant to the practice of contemporary American civil justice. I have seen the same techniques used by Powell countless times—with similar success. Of course, the courts can't always render a perfect solution. But the system we have now does not—cannot—provide real justice.

Jammed with cases and overloaded with technicalities, the system is paralyzed. Judges can't hear every case; they haven't the time. They must shuffle the cases through numbing pretrial procedures or force "compromise" upon as many litigants as possible—in an effort to dispense what limited justice they can.

So who is to blame?

Lawyers are popular targets. In a system that best serves technicality, lawyers *must* be technical. And given the realities of the system, they soon learn their best winning strategy is to exploit its weaknesses through technical attacks.

What about defendants, like Powell, who evade the legal process? These are the people who refuse service of court papers; who decline to attend hearings; who, after losing their case, simply refuse to pay; or who load their assets into a pickup truck or safe deposit box. Well, they may be partly to blame, but the system, tripping over itself, is often powerless to stop them and, in effect, rewards their efforts.

Legislators offer tempting marks, but they did not cause the legal system's failure. At the same time, they have not expanded the court system to accommodate its exploding caseload, adding, instead, more laws, more technicalities, more rules and regulations.

Where, then, shall we place the blame?

On *time*. Time is the enemy.

While there are lots of individual flaws within our system, the core issue is how they all contribute to the unmanageable chunks of time—and endless delays—that drag down cases and clients. Granted, with each step taken in prosecuting a case, numerous procedural steps can help bring clarity and ease to the process. But few of these procedures can match the overall benefits achieved when the system of law is compressed to make efficient use of time.

The goal of this book is to shine an unwavering light on the inequities that arise from time. The Sixth

Amendment of the U.S. Constitution guarantees "the right to a speedy trial" for defendants in criminal prosecutions. But what about civil cases? Where are the guarantees for speedy justice in these cases, which comprise the vast majority of disputes in our judicial system?

My goal in writing this book is to show the heartbreak and "dollar-break" of today's judicial system through the retelling and interweaving of two stories. The first story is that of *James v. Powell.* While this case took place decades ago, it remains, for me, an iconic and fascinating case study—a case that demonstrates virtually every aspect in which the civil justice system can be manipulated and distorted by time.

The second story is my own: my professional experiences as a practicing attorney, handling hundreds of cases that mirror the legacy of delay so exquisitely highlighted by the Powell case. Some of my experiences have involved prominent clients, including renowned financier Bernard Baruch; Nobel Laureate Aleksandr Solzhenitsyn; movie and TV actor Douglas Fairbanks, Jr.; adult film star Linda Lovelace; singer/songwriter Harry Chapin; pro football star Freeman McNeil; heavyweight boxing champion Gene Tunney; media mogul and America's Cup racing champion Ted Turner; and singer and *American Idol* judge Paula Abdul. Many other cases, however, involved regular people who could be your neighbors—or you. All of these cases lead to one conclusion: Justice must be sped up. The time between conflict initiation and resolution must be shortened—and shortened dramatically.

Today's legal system is a contact sport: It has evolved into a body of principles without practicality. Day by day, the people whom the law is intended to serve are losing confidence in its ability to provide justice; with each encounter they are less likely to trust the next one. In the end, the administration of civil justice takes too long; costs too much; drains us psychologically; and produces unpredictable outcomes.

When the French political thinker and historian Alexis deToqueville came to America in the early 19th century, he famously noted: "In America, I saw more than America; I saw the image of democracy itself." But the image of democracy is a reflection of our system of justice—and it is this system that is the very fabric of our culture. If we refuse to protect this system, then our democracy itself is at risk.

It's time for us to curtail the excesses of time in our legal system—and for us to make it a national priority if we are to preserve the dreams and ideals set forth by our founders.

It's about time.

1

Powell: The Fiery Congressman Sets a Blaze

It's early Sunday evening, March 6, 1960. Congressman Adam Clayton Powell, Jr., basks beneath the studio lights, posing between moving TV cameras and a team of technicians sighting the best shooting angles. The representative from Harlem's 15th Congressional District had rushed to the fourth-floor television studio in Manhattan's Times Square, but now he appears relaxed, self-assured. He glances slowly over the set; at his microphone, his interviewer, the cameraman. He smiles. He's ready. Let the show begin.

At the height of his career, Powell has become a formidable politician. In 1944 he was the first black congressman elected in New York and, in fact, the entire East Coast. Earlier he had made his mark as a young pastor of the influential Abyssinian Baptist Church on West 138th Street, succeeding his father in 1937. From the church's marble altar, Pastor Powell fired up his congregation with evangelical eloquence every Sunday, delivering stirring sermons on "day-to-day practical Christianity"—virtually any subject, political or social.

Over the years, Powell learned how to blend his religious influence and political ambitions with staggering force and personal magnetism, more effectively than any black politician had before him. Tall and handsome, he was actually so light-skinned (his paternal grandfather was white) that as an undergraduate at Colgate University he had been "rushed" by an all-white fraternity.

In New York City, then Washington, the Democratic congressman fought for equal rights for blacks, challenging practices such as the informal ban on black representatives using Capitol facilities reserved for members only. He would become chairman of the powerful House Education and Labor Committee, presiding over programs for wages and work hours, vocational training and aid to elementary and secondary education. He would send to the floor 60 of the most progressive bills of the Kennedy-Johnson era, and while he was committee chair, not one of his bills was ever defeated once delivered to the House floor.

His constituents have reseated him in Congress again and again, by huge majorities. But the King of Harlem is a star driven by a star's volatile temperament. Despite his extraordinary political career, Powell has earned a well-deserved reputation for spending less time at his job in Congress than any of his colleagues. Whether sunning at his island home in Bimini or relaxing on his high-powered deep-sea fishing boat, *Adam's Fancy*, Powell makes no effort to conceal his affection for icy tropical cocktails and alluring women.

He is an American phenomenon.

On this Sunday night in March, Lester Wolff, the producer and moderator of Channel 13's interview program, *Between the Lines*, has asked Powell to appear after presidential candidate Hubert Humphrey telephoned to say that he was trapped in Washington by foul weather. (Channel 13, now a public television station, was then the commercially owned WNTA-TV.)

From 7:00 to 7:30, Powell leads Wolff through a wide variety of topics, including one of Powell's favorites, alleged police corruption in Harlem.

"I can name names," the King declares. One of them is Esther James, a 63-year-old widow living on earnings from her late husband's railroad pension, as well as from her work as a domestic. He calls James a "bag woman"—a slang term meaning a go-between who works for corrupt police officers collecting bribes from gamblers in exchange for securing their protection from arrest.

Esther James is a heavy-set black woman whose hazel eyes, behind metal-rimmed glasses, are often accented by big-brimmed "Bella Abzug hats," famously worn by the New York City congresswoman and leader of the women's movement. James would later testify that she had been in her five-room railroad flat on Amsterdam Avenue on the evening the program was aired. She recalled that a friend telephoned that night to tell her that Powell was talking about her on television. She switched on her set in time to hear herself described as a bag woman.

James knows what it means. She's shocked. The next day, she telephones Powell's office in Washington seeking an apology. Despite repeated calls, she is never able to penetrate Powell's thick insulation of congressional aides. So Esther James decides to sue the King of Harlem.

2

Time Troubles: Everyday Justice—and Injustice

Much law, but little justice.
—Thomas Fuller, Gnomologia, *1732*

It is the spring of 2005.

One of my clients, a famous radio and TV talk show host, signs a contract to buy a house on Long Island's Gold Coast. As agreed upon, he puts down $132,500, about 5 percent of the total purchase price of $2.65 million. All seems well—the housing market is in full stride.

But within a few weeks negotiations hit a snag. The contract requires the sellers to deliver a clean title to the property. If they fail to do so, they will have to return the down payment, along with the cost of examining the title. As it turns out, there are some big problems.

After the contract is signed—and without our knowledge—the sellers enter into an agreement with their neighbors to erect a new chain link fence along their property line, in place of the existing stockade fence. The kicker: The sellers are required to maintain the fence "in good condition," and any repair or replacement would be at the sole expense of the sellers or subsequent owners of their property—in other words, my client.

A flurry of letter-writing follows between the sellers' attorney and my law firm. We cancel the sales contract and demand that the sellers return the down payment. They refuse. More letter-writing.

My client, who has worked for years in the highly visible media world, is no longer interested in the house; he wants his down payment back. We take the matter to court.

In the fall of 2005, we file a motion for summary judgment in State Supreme Court, asking the court to issue a decision in our favor, assessing the evidence without requiring a jury trial. The sellers file a counterclaim, also for a summary judgment. Several months later, the court finds in our favor and as ordered, the sellers turn over the down payment, plus interest and title costs paid to the county—but then they file an appeal to the Appellate Division. Both sides write briefs; arguments are established. The Appellate Division reverses the lower court decision.

We decide not to appeal that decision, but in the summer of 2008 we file another motion for summary judgment, seeking cancellation of the contract based on a second title defect. During the earlier title search we also had found that the tax bill for property my client is buying includes the taxes assessed for another lot that the sellers own, but it isn't part of the sale. Their real estate broker informs us that the sellers would be willing to transfer title of the other lot to my client at no cost. But in a later phone conversation, the sellers' attorney says the broker had no authority to make that offer. If the sellers agree to transfer title to the other lot, they would expect additional compensation.

Subsequently, the sellers' attorney contacts the Nassau County Department of Assessment and finds that the tax assessment of the two lots can be separated through an application to the county. As an inducement, he says, the sellers "will defend, save and hold the purchaser harmless from all tax assessments" levied against the additional lot.

Not interested, my client says. All he wants is his money back, in accordance with the terms of the contract.

The sellers also file a motion for summary judgment. Depositions are taken by both sides. In the spring of 2009, we win the motion for summary judgment. But the case may not be over. As I write this chapter, the time for appeal has not run out. We don't know whether the sellers will appeal (we expect so), or even whether the case may eventually go on to a full trial.

Four years later, my client's legal fees and costs are already $80,000.

It won't be long before the total costs eclipse the potential benefit—the recovery of the $132,500 down payment.

Welcome to everyday justice in America.

Yes, this case involves a media celebrity, but it is not an atypical case. I've handled hundreds of cases involving both celebrities and ordinary citizens, all of which have been compromised in one way or another by the time it takes to achieve justice.

Admittedly, "justice" is difficult to define in precise terms, but it's easy to describe in terms of everyday experiences. The concept is inextricably linked to the notion of "fairness," of being treated equitably by our legal system. Justice is the footing upon which our republic stands; indeed, what makes us a unified society is that we recognize certain rules as binding, and we agree to live mostly within their limits.

In his 1971 philosophical classic, *A Theory of Justice*, the late Harvard professor John Rawls observed that "justice deals with the conflicting claims upon the advantages won by social cooperation.... These principles inherently apply to relations among several persons or groups, as does the concept of a 'contract'—which also suggests the condition...that the appropriate division of advantages must be in accordance with principles accepted by all parties."

But how can we apply such lofty and elusive principles of fairness? How do we settle "conflicting claims," ensuring that the "appropriate division of advantages" is in accordance with "principles accepted by all parties"? After all, it is precisely our *inability* to agree that becomes the driving reason for going to court, as Esther James and my media star did. And presumably, it is the function of the courts, judges and lawyers to work together in an effort to transform our principles of justice from an abstract vocabulary of law into a common language of fair decisions. But is that what's happening today?

During America's infancy, our communities were small and cohesive. Townspeople shared personal as well as business relationships, based on mutual trust: If your reputation was good, it was relied upon; a handshake was your bond and contract. But if your reputation was dubious—well, others took heed. That's why swindlers and sharpies kept on the move.

After World War II, America's economy and population expanded exponentially as cities and suburbs grew. The nation's advancing computer technologies and transportation and information systems began to make the nation seem smaller and more homogeneous. But with an increasingly diverse population and accelerating change, we, as citizens, have become more isolated and anonymous.

In 1965, futurist Alvin Toffler coined the term "future shock" to describe the stress individuals and institutions would bear as modern culture surged into the 21st century. He warned that individuals would need to search out totally new ways to anchor themselves, "for all the old roots—religion, nation, community, family or profession—are now shaking under the hurricane impact of the accelerative thrust."

Mutual trust, which has been the essential ingredient in our culture's growing economic and social complexity, has all but disappeared. The result is an untrusting, litigious society reluctant to admit faith in anything.

As the nation roared through the 1960s and early '70s, we experienced massive social unrest and confrontations. The result, wrote the late Amherst professor and cultural critic Benjamin De Mott, was that "the entire articulate American community—young, middle-aged, and aged alike—was transformed into a monster of damnation-dealers, its voice pitched ever at a hysterical level, its prime aim to transform every form of discourse into a blast." These largely successful protests set a dangerous precedent: Defiance became effective when it became clear that the system lacked the administrative strength to bring disputes to conclusion.

Through the subsequent decades, this pattern of accelerating revolutions and global economic volatility, rather than the deliberate modulations of the past, has become predominant. In an effort to accommodate a growing number of complex societal relationships, the legal system has swelled with complexity. But our contemporary system of justice cannot keep up with such social and technological hyperactivity. The courts are overwhelmed, buckling under the strain; the system is no longer a predictable process.

At the first National Conference on Public Trust and Confidence in the Justice System in 1999—

sponsored by the American Bar Association and the League of Women Voters, among other advocacy groups—four top concerns emerged from discussions among the participants: the perception of unequal treatment within the justice system; the high cost of getting access; an unfair and inconsistent judicial process; and the lack of public understanding about the system.

At the same time, a poll sponsored by the National Center for State Courts found that nearly half of those surveyed said they believed that the courts were "out of touch with what's happening in their communities; that it's too costly to bring a case to court; and that everything about the process takes too much time or hassle."

Our civil justice system needs what I call a dose of Judge Judy. As most people know, *Judge Judy* is a courtroom reality TV show featuring former family court judge Judy Sheindlin, who arbitrates over small claims cases. While some critics complain about Sheindlin's gruff manner and occasional explosive "Judyisms" aimed at parties appearing in her court ("Liar, liar, pants on fire"), there is no question about her swift handling of cases. (According to the tagline, it's "A show where justice is dispensed at the speed of light.") Not surprisingly, *Judge Judy* is among several popular, long-running courtroom-themed shows today, including *The People's Court*, featuring Judge Marilyn Milian, *Judge Joe Brown* and *Judge Mathis*.

Today, the final judgment—the evaluation of the quality of "justice" the system provides—is left for you and me to decide. Our impressions are shaped by the amount of time spent in the system, our everyday experiences with government agencies and courts and our involvement in lawsuits as plaintiffs, defendants, jurors, witnesses and observers.

Ultimately, the judicial system is not only a tool for society; it is also its teacher. And what it has taught us—as Esther James learned years ago—is that simply being buttressed by myriad laws and administrative procedures does not equip a legal system to deliver justice. If such a system does not judiciously control the time required to resolve disputes, in our age of 24/7 global business, it cannot succeed—or survive.

3

Powell: The Chase Begins

The first task Esther James faces is finding an attorney—one willing to take on the King of Harlem. She goes to a Wall Street law firm, but the pinstriped attorneys there turn her away. "Not our kind of case," they say.

Four months after the "bag woman" statement was broadcast, James makes an appointment to see Raymond Rubin, a shirt-sleeved lawyer who practices alone in an office on the corner of Broadway and Chambers Street. James had read stories about him in several black-oriented publications. One cited a $20,000 judgment he had wrested from the former prizefighter, Sugar Ray Robinson, whose dog had gnawed one of Rubin's clients. Another article noted a $75,000 judgment Rubin had won for a black youth maimed by an explosion in a factory.

This *is* Rubin's kind of case.

So on July 28, 1960, the lawsuit *James v. Powell* officially begins when complaints are served on the Harlem Democrat, the NTA Television Broadcasting

Company and the Associated Food Stores, the program's sponsor.

Thus commences one of the classic cases in the history of modern jurisprudence. It isn't like other landmark trials you learn about in law school—such as Nuremburg, Scopes, Miranda—that established great truths or precedents. In its substance, the Powell case examines no profound social question; it defines no legal principle that would alter the code of society; it isn't studied by legions of aspiring attorneys every year. The facts of this case are not publicly debated. But *James v. Powell* will reveal an ominous truth in its turbulent and lengthy life in the courts: Delays, defiance and complex administrative procedures can inject so much time into a routine case that there is little hope for *real* truth or justice.

When James initiates her lawsuit, she has no idea of the court system's many weaknesses. Rubin, in fact, is so confident he will win that he represents James on a contingency fee basis—an arrangement where a percentage of the final judgment is given the attorney rather than his receiving a fee based upon an hourly rate. Thus, Rubin essentially becomes an economic partner in the case.

In 12 years of relentless legal pursuit, the lawyer will gamble thousands of hours of his time in court and in preparing motion papers for James's case; he will also invest several thousands of dollars of his own money to cover out-of-pocket expenses. But neither he nor James anticipates the bold resistance Powell and his lawyers will mount. Neither imagines their complete helplessness to conclude the case—long after the decision of Powell's liability has been rendered.

When the news breaks that Adam Clayton Powell, Jr., is involved in a $1 million defamation-of-character suit, hardly anyone in Harlem is startled.

The story in the *Amsterdam News*, the oldest black-owned newspaper in the United States, carries the headline: "Ho Hum, They're after Adam again." In the past, "they" had included rival politicians, the Internal Revenue Service, two former wives trying to collect alimony and fellow representatives in the House. He was a tested veteran in deflecting the system to beat his adversaries.

Within a few days of his appearance on *Between the Lines*, Powell is on trial in federal court, charged with income tax evasion. He is fighting a three-count indictment accusing him of falsifying his tax returns. Powell hires one of the country's most prominent defense lawyers, Edward Bennett Williams, as his chief counsel. Within a year, the trial ends with two charges dismissed and the jury hung on the third.

Powell has an almost laughable talent for attracting million-dollar lawsuits. Richard Jones, a lawyer whom Powell defeated in the June primary for the Democratic nomination in New York's 15th Congressional District, filed a $1 million slander-and-libel suit against Powell, accusing him of distributing "false, libelous, and defamatory attacks" upon him during the campaign. Powell treats all these cases with the same flippancy.

With the start of the defamation suit come telephoned and written threats to James and Rubin, warning them to drop their case or die. They refuse. But for years, James is afraid to leave her apartment. She often asks a neighbor to shop for her, and on several occasions receives protection from the police. During the next six years, Rubin attends many social functions and even hearings in court in the company of private detectives.

In February 1962, the television station and the program's sponsor settle with James for a total of

$1,500 and are dropped as defendants. Powell, who that month became the new chairman of the powerful House Education and Labor Committee, refuses to apologize to James or to discuss a settlement.

During the pretrial hearings, Powell's attorneys argue that his televised remarks were meant to inform his constituents of a speech he had made earlier on the floor of the House. Thus, they reason, Powell should be immune from prosecution under Article I, Section 6 of the U. S. Constitution that states that "...for any speech or debate in either House, they [Senators or Representatives] shall not be questioned in any other place."

Rubin responds that Powell's immunity should not be extended to his remarks on *Between the Lines*. Justice John L. Flynn of the New York State Supreme Court rules on July 6, 1962, that "a legislator has a qualified privilege of informing his constituents of remarks made by him in Congress so long as the communication to the constituents is made in good faith and without malice." But he adds that a hearing is needed to determine whether Powell's televised statement "went beyond the limits of qualified privilege and was maliciously made."

What exactly did Mr. Powell say about James and corruption within the Washington Heights police department on the floor of the House? At a later pretrial examination of Powell, Rubin tries to find out, but Powell's lawyer for the moment, Jerry J. Lipsig, protests Rubin's line of questioning. The lawyers take the dispute to Justice George M. Carney, who rules on October 8 in Powell's favor. "Even though it is claimed that the purpose in making the Congressional statement was an unworthy one," Carney declares, "the privilege is not lost."

Still, the pretrial hearings—swollen with technicalities, motions and appeals—would end up overflowing into the spring of 1963. Three years after the case began, with the trial date approaching, Powell's attorneys are talking about a possible settlement.

4

Time Troubles: The Procedural Plague

To me the law seems like a sort of maze through which a client must be led to safety, a collection of reefs, rocks and underwater hazards through which he or she must be piloted.
—John Mortimer,
Clinging to the Wreckage, *1982*

Just after noon on July 16, 1981, Harry Chapin was driving west on the Long Island Expressway in his blue Volkswagen Rabbit. It was a typical day for an atypical man. Chapin, the 38-year-old folksinger known to many as “America’s Troubadour,” was going to give a concert that evening before 30,000 fans gathered in Eisenhower Park. He was a tireless performer and often donated big chunks of his concert revenues to social and charitable causes. Chapin left his musical imprint on a generation with hits like “Taxi” and “Cat’s in the Cradle”—and he used his stardom to energize the arts on Long Island as well as to help lead the fight to end world hunger.

Harry was a lover of life—what I call “a total biophile.” He wanted to win the Nobel Peace Prize—he even talked about it. His friend, Robert Redford, marveled that he never met “anybody with the degree of energy and the degree of commitment all tied into one force like him."

But on that summer day, the unstoppable force was tragically stopped.

Chapin was driving about 65 miles an hour in the left lane when for unknown reasons (a mechanical or medical problem?) he put on his emergency flashers, slowed to 15 miles an hour and veered into the center lane, nearly colliding with another car. He swerved left, then right again, directly into the path of a tractor-trailer truck that could not brake in time. The truck rammed the back of Chapin's Volkswagen, rupturing the fuel tank. The car burst into flames.

The driver of the truck and another driver got Chapin out of the burning car, and a police helicopter took to him to the hospital where doctors vainly tried to save him. Hospital officials said Harry died of cardiac arrest, but couldn't say exactly when it occurred.

In the ensuing months, Chapin's stunned family members spent many thousands of dollars trying to establish the proximate cause of Harry's death. They retained experts from many disciplines; seldom has there been so much work done at such high cost in preparing for an auto accident case.

As attorney for the Chapin family, I ended up filing a complaint for negligence against both Supermarkets General, the owner of the truck, and Volkswagen. Among other things, the suit alleged that Chapin would have survived the accident if Volkswagen had engineered the car he was driving more safely. More specifically, Volkswagen of America had manufactured an unsafe seat belt mechanism—and knew it.

This was a unique case: an international auto giant against an international star's family—millions at stake, as well as reputations. It's far easier and less costly to prove the other driver's negligence. But to take on the safety record of Volkswagen—that's a serious decision. For VW, this suit wasn't just about Harry's death. If the case went against Volkswagen, the company could potentially be liable for all the cars out there that had this type of seat belt and be forced by a court decision to make improvements in all those cars.

The Chapin family knew the company would be a formidable opponent and that litigation would mean many years of legal fighting, motions by the score, conferences, depositions, court rulings, jury selections, weeks in trial and then—even if successful—appeals and perhaps going back to trial. It would take endurance; it was a fight without an end in sight. Still, the family felt a strong sense of social responsibility—they wanted to get some value out of the death of Harry. Following in the footsteps of Ralph Nader in his campaign against the construction of the Corvair in his book *Unsafe at Any Speed*, the Chapins decided that this would be a battle to help make cars safer.

In this case, the critical issue was Volkwagen's seat belt. The company had changed the seat belt configuration in the VW Rabbit so that it went only over Chapin's shoulder, not his lap. The shoulder strap was effective in stopping injuries resulting from front-end crashes—it prevented the body from heading into the steering wheel. But the lap seat belt, our experts told us, was absolutely essential in keeping the driver in his seat if the vehicle were hit from behind.

What killed Harry, we believed, was that when he was hit from behind by the truck, his head and torso moved back, and because the seat was not strong enough to keep him sitting upright (without a lap seat belt) his body ramped up in the seat. As his head hit the overhead, his torso moved out of the protective area of the seat, causing his body to snap violently, rupturing his aorta and resulting in almost instantaneous death.

That case was categorically strong, but the family knew it would be hard fought on every element—the counsel for Volkswagen was an astute litigator who contested every case assiduously, with every legal procedure. Before the trial commenced, the Chapin family decided to drop Volkswagen as a defendant, focusing instead on Supermarkets General, which had a capable but less daunting legal team.

The decision to drop Volkswagen as a defendant was based almost solely on time: the road was too long and uncertain, and the resultant cost too high. Here was a chance to expedite the case, move it along, and be fairly certain that there wouldn't be further litigation.

Undoubtedly, the decision cut years off the case. A jury did award the Chapin family $10.57 million in damages for the truck driver's negligence—although it *was* seven years after Harry's death.

The Chapin case—like the Powell case decades before it—demonstrates how time-consuming procedural strategies and tactics have exploded. Pre- and posttrial skirmishes—the motions, hearings, discovery proceedings—have now become formalized and extended, quickly outgrowing even the periods of delay that had originally invited their development. More and more cases have bogged down in the mire of time.

The customary procedural elements of the law have developed a new and burgeoning significance. No longer are these precursory actions mere formalities that resolve questions of evidence and jurisdiction before trial. Increasingly, lawyers have come to realize that failure at any of the procedural stages could cripple a case or expel it from the court.

The procedural plague has been with us for some time. More than 30 years ago, judicial, legal and academic leaders gathered to reconsider the issues raised by the famed legal scholar Roscoe Pound in his

1906 address to the American Bar Association entitled "The Causes of Popular Dissatisfaction with the Administration of Justice." At the outset of the conference, then-U.S. Supreme Court Justice Warren Burger noted that Pound had called the court system "archaic" and court procedures "behind the times" and wasteful of judicial time—and that was more than 100 years ago.

The process today still tends to uphold form over substance. Has "notice" of the suit been properly composed and properly delivered? Has the plaintiff appealed to the proper courts? Within the proper period of time?

Originally, the reasons for these technical rules were noble—in the interests of fairness. They were designed to protect individual rights. In the Powell case, for example, we will see that the rule of proper service of a subpoena was intended to ensure that a defendant is given proper notice of an action being initiated against him. But in recent years this ideal has become obscured by the game.

Today, landlord-tenant law is just one area that is frequently littered with procedural quagmires. An example:

While a young woman is away for the weekend, a severe spring storm soaks through the ceiling of her apartment, ruining a shelf full of books and the living room carpet. Since the preceding October, she had repeatedly asked her landlord to fix the roof. Once she had even threatened to withhold the rent. In return, he threatened to keep her $3,000 security deposit and have a sheriff throw her out. She backed off.

Finally reaching her breaking point, she hires an attorney and turns to the courts. Her lawyer maps out her strategy and serves a summons and complaint. She waits patiently. But after three or four months, she wonders why the case is moving so slowly. The landlord's attorney demands a Bill of Particulars, claiming, "I don't understand exactly what you mean by your complaint.

Please explain it to me more clearly so that I can answer it." After the woman's attorney further explains the complaint in a Bill of Particulars, the landlord's attorney studies it for as long as he is allowed. Afterwards, he still isn't "quite sure" of the tenant's allegations and calls the first Bill of Particulars "defective"; he wants another. Motions flutter over the bench. Motions that the landlord has not answered the complaint in a timely fashion and thus he should be judged in default. Motions for further Bills of Particulars. Motions and cross-motions.

Months later, the substance of the complaint is at last established and formally answered, and the next pretrial phase begins. The tenant's attorney requires documents from the defendant to prepare her case, so he applies for them in a discovery proceeding. He makes a motion before the court to discover the records and contracts he needs. After a period of reflection, the landlord's attorney responds that the law does not require his compliance with the motion. The tenant's attorney replies, "Oh, yes, the law does require compliance!"

The disagreement now rests with the court until the judge can render his decision: "motion granted." Eventually, the landlord hands over assorted documents—with certain records missing. The woman's lawyer files more motions with the court. As the suit staggers on, we see two things happening. Not only is the tenant's case being hurt by the system's inability to respond, but her case, in turn, is further weakening the court's ability to provide timely justice in other cases. Meanwhile, her furnishings are being destroyed. The system, stalled by the landlord's evasions and defiance, spews out delays and grinds the tenant's sense of justice into cynicism. It devours energy, opportunity, money and time—months and even years—until her will is exhausted and the case is thus "settled."

* * *

Time Fixes

*** Eliminate pretrial paperwork**

Overall, the strategy most crucial to streamlining justice is to remove procedures from paperwork, whenever possible. The mass production of legal documents only buries judges, busies lawyers, generates delays and costs money. It does not promote justice.

Instead of swamping the court in legal documents, both litigants and their attorneys should come before their assigned judge immediately after notice is served and talk the preliminary issues through. There need be no endless exchange of written bills and motions. In front of the judge and the court's stenographer, one can simply ask the other to clarify certain parts of the complaint or answer certain other questions. The discussion would continue, with the judge's assistance, until both sides thoroughly understood the issues in dispute.

Of course, the judge could periodically adjourn to provide the attorneys time to research legal questions or to produce materials requested by their opponent. But no so-called misunderstandings, either genuine or feigned, would be left unsettled to devour time later in the case. When all the preliminary issues have been discussed and settled, the judge would immediately set a date for trial.

*** Modify service notification procedures**

Today, we must not only notify the defendant in various proceedings; we must notify him only in certain ways prescribed by the law. If we deviate from the law's requirement for proper notice, then as far as the court is concerned, the defendant has not been notified at all and the proceeding must be annulled or adjourned. The defendant's lawyer can adroitly argue: "I am in court today, your Honor, only to argue that I don't have to be here, because the notice of the proceedings was technically flawed."

Perhaps the subpoena *was* mistakenly delivered by certified mail, or perhaps the document listed an inaccurate address; whatever the error, the defendant was improperly notified of his scheduled appearance in court. Often the whole process of notification must then be repeated—and perhaps yet again—until the attorneys for the defense can contrive no more technical objections.

Before any court can begin hearing a lawsuit, the defendant must be properly notified by the plaintiff that he is being sued and must be given fair opportunity to prepare a defense. These rights to proper notification are guaranteed by the Constitution in its due process clause. So the right to notice is an essential first step toward justice.

But with modern mobility and the mire of procedural law constantly thickening, the plaintiff is now unfairly burdened with the task of "properly" notifying the defendant of the upcoming suit. According to procedural guidelines, an individual may legally notify another of an impending suit by personal or "substituted" service. Each form is meticulously prescribed by statute, and the law insists on perfection in every detail. The spirit of the rules of notice is lost in a preoccupation with technicalities

Yet notice must be ensured. The best way to save time getting a suit started is not to concoct more elaborate legal procedures, but to shift some responsibility from the plaintiff to the defendant. The plaintiff must be required to compose his complaint and summons properly and file them with the proper court. But instead of the present arrangement, every person liable for suit by another should be made responsible to an address and be required to monitor that address for service of a legal notice. The plaintiff would be required only to prove that he delivered the notice to the defendant's address. Then, within a prescribed period of time, the defendant would have to answer the complaint.

While many might wince at the suggestion of a national or statewide system of registration, whether voluntary or mandatory, such registration need not threaten our privacy. After all, most of us already have an official address—recorded with the Internal Revenue Service; Social Security; state departments of motor vehicles and taxation; numerous other agencies of local, state and federal governments; our employers, landlords and creditors.

Far from a threat to our freedom, the system would in the long run strengthen our system of justice by saving time and money. Such a system is actually our only reasonable alternative to adopting a strong-arm approach to justice. A plaintiff today can hardly serve notice upon an evasive defendant. As our society inevitably becomes even more complex, how will our courts and legislators respond? Giving courts more police power to punish evasion is the most obvious solution—but it is also a dangerous one.

Participation in this system of notice need not be mandatory; a voluntary system would work well. Before entering into a business deal a person may ask, "Are you registered for service in this state?" Both parties, by registering for service, would guarantee their legal presence and thus demonstrate their good faith. Eventually, this registration would become a standard of credibility and help speed cases by eliminating most arguments challenging a court's jurisdiction over the parties.

In addition to ensuring acceptance of notice, we must ensure its proper delivery to a person's address. Currently, the notice of a pending lawsuit is usually delivered by a professional process server, who is paid by the plaintiff's attorney. These servers are always paid more money for success than for failure, so some deliverymen try to minimize the record of unsuccessful attempts by claiming to serve the documents but never actually doing so. This has come to be known as "sewer service," meaning that the summons could just as well have been thrown down a sewer—even with the process server later swearing that he had handed the papers to the defendants and sent another copy to them through the mail. But postal records do not certify that the envelope delivered actually contained the notice; the envelope may have been stuffed with yesterday's newspaper.

As professional process servers' "efficiency" improves, their profits may soar, but so may default judgments, resulting from defendants' failure to receive service. (In New York, this problem spurred a wide-ranging investigation of possible fraud in the process-serving industry in the spring of 2009.) To repair this problem, we must extract private process servers from the legal network; instead, the court should take responsibility. The plaintiff's attorney should prepare the summons, compose the complaint and submit it to the court, whose clerks would verify its content and mail it to the party's registered address.

5

Powell: The Verdict Clips a King—or Does It?

On April 1, 1963, the trial opens in State Supreme Court before Justice Thomas A. Aurelio.

Powell is not in the courtroom. Charles T. McKinney, one of his lawyers, says the congressman is extremely busy in Washington and therefore not able to attend the trial—but he would visit the court at a later date to speak in his own defense.

Rubin introduces his elderly client as a "church-going woman, a woman of good reputation." She has never been associated with gamblers, he says. In fact, she has often told police about "policy racketeers" who operate in her neighborhood in the Washington Heights section of Harlem. Assistant Chief Inspector James Nidd, the commanding officer at the Manhattan West Precinct at the time Powell's interview was telecast, later verifies James's cooperation with the police.

McKinney declines to present an opening statement for the defense. James then takes the stand. Her eyes filling with tears, she testifies that she had been fired from her job as a domestic two days after the broadcast and had since had trouble locating work. A neighbor, Ruby Jane Elliott, testifies that most residents of Harlem believe that "if Adam Clayton Powell said James was a 'bag woman,' it must be true. I have seen people spit at her."

When the first day of the trial ends, Powell offers James $10,000, but no apology. She flatly refuses his offer. No apology, no deal.

At noon of the second day, Rubin rests his case.

McKinney moves to dismiss the suit. Motion denied. The lawyer then admits that none of his witnesses are prepared to take the stand and he requests an adjournment.

"I will give you no more time," Justice Aurelio snaps from the bench. "If you're not ready, I'll have to submit the case to the jury." But shortly afterward, Aurelio relents to McKinney's plea that he be allowed to defend Powell later that day.

When the justice restarts the trial, Powell's attorney is ready. He begins by calling Odel Clark to the witness stand. Clark serves as chief investigator for Powell's House Education and Labor Committee and is a co-leader with Powell of the Alfred E. Isaacs Democratic Club. Through the club, Clark says, he has fielded "certain complaints...about one Esther James."

Aurelio quickly silences the investigator by announcing that such testimony can be presented only by its source, not second-hand.

Clark then describes his mission for Powell: follow up on the complaints. Before long, the investigator had unearthed the complainants and had each of them sign an affidavit affirming his respective complaint. Their names are Harleston ("Cool Breeze") Patterson and Paul Moore. Clark does not further identify the two men.

When the second day of the trial ends, Powell makes another offer to James: $10,000 and a formal apology. Too late. By that time, Rubin feels he has torn apart Powell's defense witnesses and can get his client (and himself) a much better dollar judgment from the jury. He is right.

On the third day the huge trial audience overflows the courtroom. Powell's fans pack the court and mill about anxiously in the adjacent corridor. More wait outside on Foley Square's courthouse steps—as well as photographers, TV cameramen, reporters—all hoping for a glimpse of the King.

Inside the courtroom McKinney calls the day's premiere witness, "Cool Breeze" Patterson, who admits that he has earned eight convictions as a so-called policy operator around Washington Heights. He describes the alleged agreement with James that he and his business partner pay her $20 per week for protection from arrest.

McKinney's second witness is Carlos Duran, who claims that he had paid James $25 per week to ensure that no police would visit his card room in Manhattan. Later, James raised her price to $50 per week, he says.

Esther James denies all charges.

In his summation, McKinney argues that, based upon his witnesses' testimony, the jurors must conclude that Powell's "bag woman" label was essentially accurate. Besides, as a congressman, Powell is still entitled to a defense of "qualified privilege," as Justice Flynn had maintained in July 1962. And even if Powell's televised remarks strayed from his speech in the House, the Congressman was addressing a topic of genuine public concern and therefore *still* deserved "qualified privilege."

By mid-afternoon, McKinney rests his case. No sight of Powell.

Then it is Rubin's turn to call rebuttal witnesses. Seizing the moment, he booms, "Your Honor, I call

Adam Clayton Powell, Jr.!"

Justice Aurelio peers over the bench to address McKinney. "Is he in New York?" the judge asks McKinney.

"Your Honor, I'm not under any obligation to tell. Mr. Rubin has the power of subpoena."

"His power of subpoena does not extend outside New York," Aurelio points out. "Mr. Rubin has depended upon your promise that Powell would be here."

Aurelio decides to excuse Powell's absence—for now. But he later reminds the jurors that they could freely interpret the congressman's absence.

On the morning of April 4, 1963, Aurelio delivers his charge and gives the case to the jury. Before the jury retires to decide Powell's fate, Rubin asks the judge to stipulate to the jurors that Powell's qualified privilege is not relevant to his case. Rubin argues that because Channel 13's program had reached far beyond Powell's congressional district, his statement could not be misconstrued as a "report to his constituents"; instead, it was merely a general public statement.

McKinney jumps to his feet.The range of Powell's audience is not crucial, he objects. For qualified privilege Powell needed only to speak on a matter of the public's concern.

"That's right," Aurelio replies, without elaboration.

The jury deliberates for four hours. The foreman hands up the verdict: Adam Clayton Powell is judged liable and fined $11,500 to compensate Esther James for damages to her reputation and earning power. Aurelio had instructed the jury to subtract $1,500 (the settlement James had received from the NTA Broadcasting Corporation and Associated Food Stores) from whatever award they might grant her in compensatory damages.

But the jury also decides that Powell had maligned James wantonly and maliciously. A suitable punishment, they unanimously agree, would be $200,000. It was an immense judgment at the time, more likely a reflection of the jurors' distaste for Powell's arrogance and his absence at the trial. The jury has fired to kill.

Blasting the verdict as "excessive and against the weight of the evidence," McKinney moves to set aside the jury award. Motion denied, Aurelio says.

After the trial, several jurors remark that Powell's failure to appear had figured into their decision. "She was here, we had to be, so why wasn't Powell?" one of the jurors says. Powell, in Washington, says only that he will appeal the verdict.

James, sitting beside her lawyer when the foreman announces the verdict, weeps with joy. "I was afraid of the King of Harlem," she says, "but I found out this is America." She says she plans to invest some of the award in property and donate the rest to the care of "crippled Jewish children." Later, an exultant Esther James repeats to reporters over and over, "The King of Harlem is dead; Adam Powell is finished."

But the King is not dead—far from it.

6

Time Troubles: The Calculus of the Courts

There are two men whom you should never go to court against unless you are dragged there: One is he who has more money than you have, and the other is he who has no money at all. With the former you may lose even if you are in the right, and with the latter you will lose even if you win.
—K. J. Back, "Law," The Royal Toast, *1920*

I first encountered Bernard Baruch at his South Carolina estate in the spring of 1965. He was in his mid-90s; I was in my mid-20s. It was a daunting experience.

I was ushered into Baruch's bedroom, where the room temperature was in the high 80s, yet Baruch was dressed in a full suit and vest, with a shawl over his shoulders. He was sitting up in bed. His eyes were a brilliant blue; his clip-on spectacles sat on the bridge of his nose. The bed was elevated, almost like an altar. And he was reading a book: a dog-eared copy of his own autobiography.

At the time, Baruch had long been a world-renowned financier, an adviser to presidents and industry titans. By the age of 30, he had earned tens of millions of dollars through the international arbitraging of gold prices—using a Marconi wireless communication device to find the pricing of gold in Europe and arbitrage the transactions to the United States. His father was a Civil War physician who pioneered hydrotherapy treatment for Confederate soldiers injured in battle.

Perched before Baruch on that spring morning, I felt insecure, uncomfortable—I was seated in a huge, wing-backed chair and my feet couldn't touch the floor. Like all the furniture in the room, the chair was oversized. Baruch was a tall man—well over six feet—and since his home was near the heart of the nation's furniture industry, he had his furniture custom-made.

Baruch began to tell me about his palatial estate named Hobcaw Barony—more than 17,000 acres fronting the Atlantic Ocean and several rivers. This was his winter residence, where his family maintained roots even after they moved to New York City. (Native Americans called the land *hobcaw*, meaning "between the waters.") At this vast plantation, Baruch hosted many important meetings in the 1940s as World War II was winding down, inviting Franklin D. Roosevelt and Winston Churchill there to discuss the future of the western alliance.

There was a road, U.S. 17, that separated the Baruch estate from an equally large Arcadia plantation owned by another iconic American family, the Vanderbilts. It was a symbolic as well as a physical divide between two powerful and fiercely competitive families. U.S. 17 ran into an old two-lane bridge that traversed a river, beyond which was the seaside city of Georgetown. The bridge was in severe disrepair, and state officials had decided to build a new four-lane bridge. But since the old bridge was essential, the new bridge and connecting road had to be built alongside it—and that's where things got dicey.

On the surface, this was an issue of "condemnation," in which the party that lost property as a result of the relocation of the road and bridge would be compensated by the government for the value of the land—although the property owner might argue in court that the award wouldn't truly compensate him for the loss. If the new road and new bridge ran east of the existing road, then Baruch would own both sides of the road frontage. However, if the road and new bridge were built to the west of the existing road, then the Vanderbilts would have frontage on both sides of the road and Baruch's property would be blocked from the bridge—not the outcome he wanted.

At first, I was perplexed that Baruch would ask me to represent him in this matter. Clearly, he had the legal recourse (and the financial resources) to take the case to court. And I wasn't a litigator, although I had come highly recommended by the president of U.S. Trust Company at the time. My area of expertise was in tax and charitable foundation issues.

I asked Baruch how we could possibly affect the state's decision as to where officials would place their bridge. As Baruch began to speak, he touched the side of his nose with his right index finger—it was a gesture I would come to recognize in the course of subsequent conversations. Whenever he wanted to say something important, privately, he would touch the side of his nose. For me, it was a gesture that evoked the image of Santa Claus—old St. Nicholas—touching his nose in "The Night Before Christmas," revealing some important secret.

"Why don't you tell them," Baruch said to me, "that if they decide to construct the bridge on the east side—my side—then upon my passing this property will be directed to the University of South Carolina for perpetual use in environmental studies."

Now I understood. There was a tax incentive in Baruch's strategy, but there was also something deeper—a determined decision to *avoid* litigation that could have taken years. Baruch wanted to resolve the issue while he was alive and to personally influence the outcome. This had nothing to do with money; it was about saving time.

Baruch could have filed suit against the state, seeking damages based on the diminished value of his property caused by the government's moving of the road. Instead, he decided to trade the value of the land for the opportunity to deliver it into an environmental trust—with the certainty that this decision would be promptly done. To expedite this solution, he needed to move fully outside the judicial system. This also would essentially block the Vanderbilt family from any countermove, since they would have to take legal action against a charitable trust—rarely a rewarding prospect.

In the end, I was able to secure a favorable settlement from the state on Baruch's behalf. Today, the Belle W. Baruch Foundation (named for his daughter) is a nonprofit organization and owner of the 17,500-acre wildlife refuge, Hobcaw Barony, where the University of South Carolina has a long-term research facility. Baruch got his tax deduction and avoided time-consuming litigation altogether, resolving the matter in weeks instead of years. And, oh, yes, he managed to tweak the nose of the Vanderbilts.

In the legal system today, time certainly costs money. But as Baruch pointedly demonstrated, the passage of time has much greater consequences. When court actions take too long, they divert claims into peripheral and inconsequential issues; distort people's recollections and testimony; and, most of all, force people to wait before a wrong is righted—without having any idea what and when the resolution will be. The questions, "How long will this take?" and as a result, "How much will it cost?" (in dollars, as well as in terms of disruption of life and lost opportunities) are the principles that govern most legal actions in America today.

To understand time's impact on justice, consider this comparison: What would it be like to have a tooth pulled over a 24-hour period or a broken bone set over several days? Unthinkable! Yet, we have no problem letting our legal system grind us into dust, dragging us through an emotionally harrowing and financially stunning experience, unpredictable in every regard except one: It takes time, lots of time.

We've developed the mythical notion that in order to be good, justice has to be slow, but history is filled with instances of speedy and effective justice. Our legal system must be deliberate, but it is not just a compilation of rules. The law must have proportionality; it must be tempered to fit human needs.

Imagine if the Scopes "Monkey Trial"—the famed 1925 trial challenging the Tennessee ban on teaching the theory of evolution—took place today. That landmark case was concluded in days; if it were tried today, the court could easily take several years to complete the trial phase alone, with testimony from experts representing all sects of religion and branches of science. All to what end? Have we equated consuming time and money with fair play?

With mounting delays, of course, the cost of justice soars. Foremost in a litigant's legal expenses is the lawyer's fee. In many metropolitan areas, that fee can easily climb to $400 an hour or more—and that does not include disbursements for telephone calls, printing, stenographic fees and investigative costs, all of which run into thousands of dollars.

Even if you are a stubborn litigant, you may be cowed by the uncertainty of your case's outcome. It has become impossible to predict the cost and time for your case with any accuracy. Now every case must be fought on two battlefronts. One is the courtroom, where attorneys wage classical legal warfare. The other is the pre- and posttrial arena, where modern "justice" has so often been decided.

Ironically, in the Powell case, the jurors virtually assured James of a long legal fight by setting the congressman's penalty so high. Balancing the cost of a legal siege against the payment of a $200,000 award (more than $1.4 million in today's dollars), Powell was sure to resist the judgment for a long time. Eventually, Powell must have calculated, James would have to compromise or wind up with little more than legal expenses. Perhaps one of Powell's lawyers would contrive some obscure technicality, providing the King with a clean escape from having to pay any punitive award. And if not, Powell could allege that he spent all his money on legal fees and had none left to pay the judgment.

Today, cases are routinely delayed for several years before they come to trial. This pretrial arena may be filled and billed with thousands of hours of procedures and investigations to discover facts of the case; eliminate or reduce the strength of allegations; and essentially set the parameters of the suit, thus establishing expectations of success or failure. And it costs lots of money—for both sides.

Just how much is "lots"? Ah, there's the rub.

Until you receive your final bill, you do not—cannot—know or predict. Like a dazed traveler, you wander with your lawyer from one legal proceeding to the next. With so many crucial hurdles to overcome before the lawyer can conclude your case, he or she finds it ever harder to give you a reasonable forecast of time. Lawyers can foresee neither the procedural roadblocks that the opposing side may construct nor the tangential issues and appeals that must be resolved before the primary issue can be debated.

In the months and years that inevitably slip by, your lawyer's fee can multiply at an ungovernable rate. Hiring an attorney to prosecute one's case has become an option only for those who can afford it and for those whose claim is big enough to cover the lawyer's fee and leave a worthwhile chunk left over. For all others—that is, most Americans—such professional help is usually impractical and not cost-effective. Even the American Bar Association has admitted that while 40 million poor Americans have access to free legal services through a number of governmental programs, "the middle 70 percent of our population is not being served adequately by the legal profession."

One alternative is to plead your own case in court, without an attorney's help. But how real is this alternative?

Several years ago, the *New York Times* reported the plight of a Brooklyn housewife who tried such a do-it-yourself approach. Her home had been damaged by a construction firm, but when she demanded that the company repair the house, the firm denied responsibility. Another contractor estimated the repairs would cost $2,800, so she decided to sue the original company for that amount.

Her first move was to search for professional help. She found it, but she also discovered that it was unaffordable. The lawyers she interviewed told her that the time necessary to handle the case would require a fee of $1,500. Undeterred, the woman resolved to fight her own case.

After five months of litigation and four appearances in court, the woman was extraordinarily lucky; she won. Or did she? The court granted her a judgment for only $495. And the lawyers representing the contractor's insurance company threatened to appeal the verdict. At the time the article was written, the beleaguered woman was unsure whether she could go on fighting. She had not had to sacrifice many days away from her work, but how much longer would the case continue? How many more days would she have to take off from work before it hurt her ability to make a living? Would she be successful on appeal? The dispute had already dragged on for 17 months, and even if she avoided every subtle legal snare along the way, would her final award really compensate her for the time, money and energy her case would yet require?

Who conspired to deprive this woman of justice? Was it the attorneys, who required a $1,500 retainer—three times her awarded judgment? No, the lawyers she consulted are not to blame; lawsuits like hers often take many months and few attorneys could have afforded to accept her case for less than $1,000. In fact, many lawyers attempt to make justice more affordable by charging too little, only to find themselves in a hole financially and unable to give each case adequate attention—inevitably angering their clients.

Simply put, this woman's rights, in dollars, were not worth enforcing if she had to pay lawyers. Even if she represented her own interests, is the value of her own time worth the financial outcome?

Most people think that if they throw enough money at a case, they can buy justice. Not so. Had this litigant been wealthy and willing to pay high fees, and take more time from her work, she probably would have won little more for her added expense and inconvenience. Civil justice today favors neither the wealthy nor the prominent. In fact, the current system favors big cases, where lots of money is at stake. But because most cases involve relatively small amounts of money, the time—and resultant cost—of litigation guarantees no justice for all.

In other cases, no amount of money solves the problem because the system can't deliver justice on time.

For example, several years ago, a young high school graduate, Steven, planned to attend New York University. A month before registration, he visited his mother's brother, Ray. When Steven's parents divorced, a fund of $20,000 had been set aside for his education and entrusted to his uncle for management and disbursal.

Ray had not gotten along with his sister, Rachel, since the divorce and vented his dislike on her son, Steven. When Steven requested his money for tuition, Ray cut the boy off and accused him of conspiring with his mother to spend the money on things other than his education. Steven produced a pre-registration receipt from the school's registrar; his uncle dismissed it as a forgery.

Rachel tried to persuade her brother to give her son money for tuition, first arguing, then pleading—all to no avail. As the deadline for payment approached, Rachel called her lawyer and filed a lawsuit.

It was a simple case. The court recognized Steven's rights and directed the uncle to pay the money. Unfortunately, the decision took three months and by then the deadline for payment had long passed. Steven missed the start-of-the-year sequence of courses he wanted and had to wait until the following fall to begin his studies. For him, justice had come too slowly to be of much value. Legal fees were $1,000.

* * *

Time Fix

*** Broadly expand the court system**

In order for the courts to handle many more cases within a reasonable time—and at the same cost—we need to physically enlarge its administrative structure. The judicial case volume has been increasing for decades, while little improvement has been made in the court system's structure.

In U.S. district courts, for example, there were about 92,000 cases commenced in 1971; in 2005 almost 279,000 cases were filed, and although about 261,000 cases were disposed, there were another 281,000 cases pending.

In 2005, about 16.7 million civil cases were filed in state trial courts; about 14 million cases were disposed but millions of cases were pending. The millions of civil cases that enter our court system each year vary widely, from lawsuits as small as $250 for, say, a dress damaged by a dry cleaner to class action suits such as the case claiming billions of dollars in damages for the adverse health effects allegedly caused by Merck's arthritis drug, Vioxx.

Furthermore, as case volume has grown, judicial salaries have not kept pace with inflation. Supreme Court Chief Justice Roberts noted in his 2008 year-end report that the federal judiciary's budget of $6.2 billion represented 0.2 percent of the total U.S. budget. "Two-tenths of 1 percent!" Roberts exclaimed. "That is all we ask for one of the three branches of government—the one charged 'to guard the Constitution and the rights of individuals,'" he wrote, quoting Alexander Hamilton.

It's time we finally came to terms with the stark facts: Our nation's courts, designed largely to resolve property rights in an agrarian era, are struggling to perform in a global, high-tech age with human rights and commercial issues ever growing in number and complexity. The court system is part of our nation's essential infrastructure. Like our roads and bridges, it simply can't support the traffic using the system today. The courts are antiquated, in need of a modernizing of their procedures, staffing and processes; otherwise they'll collapse.

Ultimately, we need to enlarge the administrative capacity of the system—perhaps by as much as 10 times—to manage in a timely way the volume of civil cases that enters the court system today. The court system must be large enough to dispose of procedures fast enough to reinforce "good behavior" by participants. Conversely, a system that allows demoralizing delays to accommodate case volume is not acceptable.

7

Powell: First Lessons From an Artful Dodger

As promised, Powell files an appeal of the jury verdict with the Appellate Division of the State Supreme Court. Rubin, getting impatient, advises State Supreme Court Justice Abraham J. Gellinoff that Powell has paid none of the judgment. He also delivers a sheriff's report stating that the officer was unable to seize any of Powell's assets to satisfy the judgment. Finally, Rubin pleads with Gellinoff to issue a civil arrest order "without notice to the defendant, Powell."

Gellinoff refuses. Powell, the judge asserts, had not demonstrated conclusively that he is evading the service of the legal papers. The justice adds, however, that Rubin could reapply for the order after notifying either Powell or his lawyer of the request.

Rubin's next tactic is to obtain a court order from State Supreme Court Justice George Postell, summoning Powell to a court hearing on June 24. There, he would be forced to explain to the judge why he should not be arrested for failing to pay the $211,500 judgment.

Three days later, James files an affidavit in State Supreme Court, accusing Powell of concealing his whereabouts and staying out of New York on weekdays "with intent to evade service of the lawful process." That is, she argues that Powell is avoiding service of her legal papers by coming into New York only on Sundays.

According to state law, no one may be served with civil court orders, subpoenas and other legal papers pertaining to civil litigation on Sundays within the boundaries of that state. Although most merchants can freely conduct business on Sundays (and sell practically anything today) in New York, civil justice is ritually suspended every weekend.

Without Powell's presence, the June 24 hearing proves dull and unfruitful. Three weeks pass before Powell files an affidavit claiming that James's affidavit fails to "set forth a single fact showing that the deponent is about to depart from the State or that he is willfully evading service of any lawful process upon." He also argues that, as a congressman, he is graced by the U. S. Constitution with immunity from civil arrest while Congress is in session as well as "in going to and returning from the same."

State Supreme Court Justice Charles Marks grants Rubin and Powell's lawyers several days to submit briefs to settle Powell's demand for congressional immunity. Then, on July 22, Marks soundly quashes James's request for a civil arrest order: All members of Congress, while called to session, are constitutionally guaranteed immunity from civil arrest, he rules.

Powell's defensive dodging skills prove artful—and formidable. He can neither be arrested nor jailed until Congress recesses. And once the session is over, he could easily avoid arrest for not paying the judgment by limiting his visits to New York to Sundays—when civil law rests. Of course, that arrangement would be fine with him, since he has to visit his district only on Sundays to preach to the congregation of the Abyssinian Baptist Church.

Meanwhile, James's attorney begins another offensive in search of Powell's assets. He knows that, by law, Powell's federal salary of $30,000 cannot be garnisheed to pay the debt. But Rubin hasn't been able to find any of his assets. So he turns to the public, pleading on TV for help in tracking the congressman's wealth.

Soon after his plea, Rubin receives an anonymous tip that sends him running to the Chase Manhattan Bank branch on 57th Street and Broadway. On July 30, he serves a restraining order from State Supreme Court on the bank. He gambles—he has no idea how much of Powell's money could be hidden inside the bank's accounts, but the order, he figures, will instantly freeze all bank assets up to twice the amount of James's judgment.

He loses. The bank has none of Powell's assets.

8

Time Troubles: The Legalization of America

Lawyers are brought up with an exaggerated reverence for their system and, apart from a few, they don't see what's wrong with it.
—Tom Sargeant, Observer, *1982*

In the summer of 1980, the sailing world was riveted by another spirited contest to decide who would defend the vaunted America's Cup. The trials were off Newport, Rhode Island, and among the competitors was Ted Turner, the media entrepreneur who was skipper of the yacht *Courageous*.

During the course of the trials, Turner broke a mast; he needed an immediate replacement to compete in the trials. So he requested that the New York Yacht Club, the holder of the cup, make a backup mast available. Three years earlier, Turner had successfully defended the Cup, the oldest active trophy in international sport, with *Courageous* beating *Australia*, four wins to nil. Still, there was little affection between the established members of the genteel private club and the brash Turner, the founder of Atlanta-based CNN, whose controversial statements earned him the nickname "Mouth of the South."

Request denied.

Yacht club officials said they would not give him a reserve mast—putting him in a disastrous position, since he would be unable to get a new mast in time to compete in the next trial. I knew Turner, raced with him and shared his competitive fire. (I captained the winning yacht in the 1977 Midget Ocean Racing Club World Championship.) We immediately filed a civil action in federal court to compel our use of the mast held in reserve. The club recanted and gave him a mast.

In this case, the threat of a lawsuit brought about the results we wanted, since any protracted litigation would have thrown off the competition's scheduling and the entire regatta would have had to be canceled. The mere presence of a lawyer from New York, with the accompanying bad publicity, forced a solution.

The *Courageous* incident is a quintessential case of how the court system could not resolve an issue in a timely fashion. In this instance, the lack of a time-sensitive judicial process worked as a weapon in our favor, simply because of the immense time pressures on the regatta itself. But there is ominous legal gridlock developing, as the time inflation in the courts collides with the growing time pressures of contemporary life.

Such gridlock has been exacerbated by the exponential "legalization" of society: Tens of thousands of new civil statutes and regulations have been added over the years, without substantive remodeling of the judicial system to function as an effective regulator of societal conduct.

In the 1960s, we began to see burgeoning of civil rights laws during the time of Powell and Martin Luther King, Jr., followed by the modern feminist movement. Even after the gradual demise of support for the Equal Rights Amendment toward the end of the 1970s, the migration of women into new sectors of society, from business and media to professional sports and military service, has provided a case study of the evolution of law. Changing social norms have generated complex new questions in legal areas such as child support after divorce and the payment of alimony.

In recent years, the whole controversial sphere of reproductive rights has exploded: When do the rights of an unborn child outweigh the rights of its mother? Does the husband's right to a child ever rival his wife's right to end pregnancy? If we expect a judge to prevent a woman from aborting the fetus, should he also prevent her from subjecting the fetus to heavy doses of drugs or alcohol? How far can the courts go in determining how a prospective mother may treat her unborn child?

Such legalization has already complicated other relationships in our culture: the private company's relationship with its client; the government's with its citizens; the banker's with its customers; the home seller's with the buyer. More than ever, people are filing lawsuits to settle their differences, clogging the courts with process and paperwork. The result is what former U.S. Supreme Court Chief Justice Warren E. Burger once called "an appalling mass of litigation"—and that was more than 30 years ago. We are entrenched in the Age of the Lawsuit.

A quick sampling:

An angry father, upset that his daughter had printed his and his wife's names on her wedding invitation without first providing him a list of all her invited guests, wanted to write each guest, explaining his dissatisfaction with her marriage. As reported in the *New York Times*, he decided to teach his kid a lesson by filing a $10,000 lawsuit against her and her fiancé—the day before they were to be married.

A homeowner, having recently moved into his new house, may have trimmed 25 feet of his neighbor's 100-

foot backyard privet hedge. The debate over whose property the hedge was actually growing on barely began when the hedge lover brought suit against his new neighbor—claiming $25,000 in damages.

A high school teacher in Connecticut believed that his rapport with his students was seriously being hampered by his having to wear a necktie. The teacher wanted to leave his tie at home and sued over this "matter of principle." The case was dismissed by the Federal District Court, reinstated in the Federal Court of Appeals and finally landed in U. S. Supreme Court, where the justices voted eight to one in favor of the school board after weighing "the alleged interest in free expression against the goals of the school board in requiring its teachers to dress somewhat more formally than they might like."

The 19th century legal philosopher Frederich Savigny declared that the law has a two-fold life: first, as part of the actual community; and second, as a distinct branch of knowledge in the hands of jurists. In the community, its form was of the natural law, which matched—in principle—the jurists' law.

But natural law and jurists' law are not remotely congruent today. Average citizens have little useful understanding of jurists' law. And new laws do not cure our legal vulnerability; instead, they heighten it. As the law swells, its bulk and impenetrable complexity provide an easier field for the specialists who contrive technical maneuvers and tactics that inject more time into the system.

Indeed, many cases seem won today through good legal counsel. The "good" lawyer is a tough, single-minded combatant. His client—his cause—is right. No contrary evidence can alter his conviction. But conviction is not the only ingredient of legal success; you need court experience and special expertise.

The law is too complex for judges to maintain a thorough understanding of all branches of law. Trial lawyers have matured into specialized practitioners whose knowledge of the court tends to give them an advantage over less experienced opponents. These lawyers know how a particular court tends to interpret key rules and procedures; they understand difficult provisions of the law.

And they also know how to fight. Legendary legal scholar Roscoe Pound once called such contentiousness the "sporting theory of justice," so rooted in the profession "that most of us take it for a fundamental legal tenet." But in his historic speech to the American Bar Association in 1906 Pound also noted that "the idea that procedure must of necessity be wholly contentious disfigures our judicial administration at every point....It leads counsel to forget that they are officers of the court and to deal with the rules of law and procedure exactly as the professional football coach with the rules of the sport."

More than a hundred years later, the so-called sporting theory was updated by former Circuit Court Judge James F. Henry, at a Georgetown University conference on the current state of the judiciary. "Large or small," Henry told the conference attendees, "a suit is an argument, a fight, or an unpleasant experience that most plaintiffs and defendants would prefer to resolve and put behind them. Sooner or later the argument becomes personal. It generates unwarranted distrust, pride, greed and anger—even among business associates. Regrettably, anger and mean tactics are the trademark of too many attorneys."

In big, high-profile cases, certain lawyers or firms are often asked to represent litigants not only because of their fighting prowess but because they have influence that is central to their client's case. Indeed, it is widely accepted that certain legal problems can be managed only by a handful of firms bulging with political muscle. In this sense, the Adam Clayton Powell case offers a prime example of an artful litigant who could dodge the system not only through his own political power but also through specialists who knew how to exert political influence in the courts. Modern justice, then, tends to follow people rather than principle.

Years ago, Joseph Goulden, a Washington journalist, wrote a book called *The Superlawyers*, profiling the cadre of prominent Washington, D.C., law firms who assumed substantial "delegated power," wielding dominant influence over the government's regulatory agencies. While acting as emissaries of corporate giants, some of them "constantly violate the public statutes...subverting the Federal Government for the financial benefit of private corporate clients."

As a counterbalance, dozens of nonprofit "superwatchdogs," following in the footsteps of Ralph Nader, have emerged to help maintain a legal balance of power. But both the superlawyers and the superwatchdogs are still relatively few in number, and they don't have the resources to help everyone equally. Thus, they tend to create even more inconsistency in the system.

Of course, many litigants cannot afford high-level legal counsel at all; they find themselves helpless in a system that simply rumbles over them. Yet there are still some legal weapons available to the legally disenfranchised. One is the class action suit, in which one person sues for himself as well as for all others similarly affected by actions such as consumer fraud, environmental damage, stock manipulation, price-fixing or job discrimination. Since vast amounts of money are at stake in a class action suit, and since such cases attract great notoriety, expert legal help is easily attracted—and often handsomely paid.

In other cases, such as *James v. Powell*, a plaintiff can hire an attorney on a contingency fee arrangement, where the lawyer works for a percentage of the judgment rather than for a set fee. Theoretically, the contingency contract is designed to provide less affluent people, like Esther James, a chance to win justice without having to resort to a free but often overworked Legal Aid attorney.

If a contingency lawyer like Ray Rubin works hard (so the theory goes), he has the opportunity to win a substantial judgment and be handsomely compensated—a clear source for motivation, yes, but also a motivation to perpetuate a case in the pursuit of more money.

In such cases the lawyer's and client's interests become commingled; they are now partners. The lawyer aims not necessarily for fairness but for a big score; the litigant learns that legal success (the dollar size of the award) is related principally to his lawyer's skill and effort, not to justice. The system becomes skewed, vulnerable to time and delays. Does the contingency attorney resist settling the case because his client deserves a larger settlement—or because he wants his portion of a larger settlement and doesn't mind *their* waiting for it?

Whether contingency lawyers or fee-based counsel, legal specialists can often perpetuate a case interminably. Once again, the incentive of financial success encourages both lawyers and litigants to load down the system with time—and put justice at risk.

* * *

Time Fixes

*** Require plaintiffs to pay expenses if appeal is lost**

While many lawsuits may be labeled trivial or a nuisance by legal experts and media pundits, such characterizations are dangerous. The distinction between trivial and important simply cannot be implemented without jeopardizing individual rights. Who is to decide which cases are trivial and which merit a trial judge's attention? Another judge in another court? The significance of these swarming cases is not their triviality but the legal system's inability to dispose of them quickly.

True, some litigants use lawsuits as leverage. They recognize the potential power of a lawsuit to paralyze an adversary, costing time and money, blocking deals and sometimes blemishing reputations. These plaintiffs are not even thinking of winning; their nuisance suits would be better described as "legal extortion," since they are specifically contrived to separate people or companies from their money.

Other people may initiate lawsuits with sincere intentions, but these suits may lack legal merit. How can a legal system distinguish between this kind of suit and the nuisance case? Even if one could distinguish among the litigants' motives, the system could never fairly separate one suit from the other, nor should it try.

Everyone deserves a trial without financial obligation beyond his or her own expenses, but if a plaintiff loses the case and appeals, then he or she should then be required to pay all of the defendant's expenses—including reasonable legal fees—accrued subsequent to trial. Under this procedure, the defendant of the original case would still stand to lose time and be inconvenienced; this cannot be avoided. But at least a venial plaintiff could no longer prolong a suit without personal financial risk, past the trial level.

*** Bar percentage contingency fees**

Our legal system is founded upon an advocacy form of justice but the roles of litigant and lawyer must be kept distinct. In a contingency arrangement, the client immediately forfeits control of the case. Even if the lawyer's personal judgment is never actually twisted, the contingency scheme eventually taints his every motive.

The spectacular fees some attorneys have won in contingency cases—from $500,000 on up—also have seriously undermined the legal profession's image. After all, what other professionals "buy into" their clients' cases and charge according to their success? Contingency arrangements demote the lawyer's image from that of an officer of the court above suspicion to that of a fast-talking broker.

Everyone in this country, wealthy or poor, must be guaranteed access to justice. Many people choose the contingency deal because it appears cheaper; they don't have to put any money up front. Others are frightened into the percentage-fee arrangement by the system's unpredictable delays and costs. But the real solution is finding ways to strip time out of the legal process, so litigation would require much less money and people would be less pressured to gamble on their lawyer's success. People should be able to reasonably estimate the cost of litigation and hire an attorney at a fixed hourly rate, payable on the contingency of success.

9

Powell: The Gentleman Vanishes

Through the second half of 1963, few people in New York get a glimpse of Adam Clayton Powell—certainly no one in court. In August, Powell misses two appearances in Upper Manhattan Criminal Court to discuss a criminal summons charging him with shifting around his income to block James's attempts to collect her judgment. On September 20 Powell misses another court date in State Supreme Court where a judge awaits an explanation of the King's financial condition. Rubin declares that he will move promptly to have Powell punished for contempt of court.

But how, exactly, would Rubin punish the congressman "promptly," since it's unclear whether *anyone* can be punished promptly in our civil system? Powell surely understands that modern reality: Those who are punished in the civil system of law are generally those who don't resist it.

So in October, Powell and his wife blithely travel to Kuwait, at the Kuwaiti government's invitation. After touring the wealthy nation and the Persian Gulf, the couple skips to Madrid for two days and then returns to their home in San Juan, Puerto Rico. A few weeks later, a San Juan newspaper reports that Powell has declined to accept a subpoena addressed to him concerning the $211,500 judgment.

At the end of November, U. S. Marshal Thomas Farley reports that a show-cause order and additional papers were successfully served on Powell on November 21 in Washington, D.C. In those documents, the New York State Supreme Court orders him to explain on December 12 why he should not be judged in contempt for not paying the award. Powell, undaunted and undented, ignores the order.

Gerald Mazur, a referee for the State Supreme Court, invites Rubin and George D. Covington, another lieutenant in Powell's army of attorneys, to submit arguments pertaining to the request for Powell's contempt citation. One of several referees appointed to advise justices on crucial issues that might otherwise delay court business, Mazur will make no final judgment on these issues. He will simply report his findings to a judge, who will then issue a decision.

Covington, a defensive specialist, has been brought in to design maneuvers that can block the collection of judgments against Powell. He insists that Powell is not required to answer the contempt charge because the subpoena was improperly served upon him. The lawyer points to the statement in the show-cause order served on November 21 that a copy of the subpoena was sent by certified mail. In such instances, he noted, subpoenas could be sent by regular mail, but not by certified mail. Although the defendant may actually be notified that he must appear in court, and even if his lawyer appears in court on schedule (a convincing demonstration that the defendant was notified), the subpoena delivered by certified mail can yet be annulled, since it did not fully comply literally with the law.

Rubin pleads that the notation "certified" on the subpoena represented only a typographical error. The subpoena, he assures Mazur, had actually been sent by regular mail. Jay Tauber, the process server, testifies before the referee that he hung one copy of the subpoena on Powell's door in Harlem and mailed him another—by regular mail. Mazur believes Tauber and Rubin and declares that "no testimony or proof was offered on behalf of the defendant to indicate the service was not made or completed."

Powell, from afar, objects to the error with boiling indignation. "I find it inconceivable," he protests, "that oaths and/or affirmations can be offered to the State Supreme Court for the truth of the facts asserted therein and then be blandly withdrawn as mere oversights when found to contain material not in accord with the facts."

Supreme Court Justice Arthur Markewich is not swayed. Three days later, the judge finds Powell in contempt for failing to explain why he shouldn't be punished for not paying the judgment. The judge commands Powell either to pay James her whole award, or to appear in court on January 6, 1964, when a judge can decide his ability to pay part of the judgment. If he does not appear on January 6, he can be arrested in New York.

As it turns out, the House of Representatives is adjourned on January 6, but it reconvenes the next day, and Powell is again immune from arrest. And even if he were arrested and hustled off to jail before the first light of January 7, he would be "a prisoner with the key to the jail door in his pocket," as one court official describes him. He could "buy his freedom immediately simply by detailing his financial status to the court and adopting a 'proper attitude.'"

Covington, meanwhile, is still hunting for a technical defense. “It is my interpretation that there has to be personal service on Congressman Powell before the court can claim jurisdiction to punish him,” he announces, adding that Powell would appeal Markewich’s decision. For his part, the congressman is still brooding over the irregularity of the paperwork: “Seeking contempt proceedings is of itself a drastic remedy,” he says, “and therefore papers offered seeking to adjudge one in contempt should be as pure as Caesar’s wife—beyond reproach.”

10

Time Troubles: Uncivil Disobedience

The Law...can be civil to you
or downright criminal.
—*Keith Miles,* The Finest Swordsman in All France: A Celebration of the Cliché, *1984*

One summer day years ago, a well-dressed man dropped into a fashionable uptown jewelry store in Manhattan. After comparing several handsome wristwatches, he settled on his favorite. He paid $1,809.54 by check, took the watch and departed.

Several days later, the jeweler, Ms. White, received the man's check in the mail, returned by the bank and stamped "PAYMENT STOPPED." Angered, she mailed a collection letter demanding immediate payment. No response. She sent another letter; still no response.

August and September passed before the jeweler finally called her lawyer. In October, the lawyer sent a short-form summons and complaint to be served upon the debtor—the standard opening gambit. Weeks later, the process server reported that the debtor had been evading personal service. The attorney quickly prepared a long-form summons and complaint which, in early

November, the process server served, by substitution, upon the debtor. The lawyer filed the original summons and complaint in court; the defendant had 30 days to answer. By certified mail, the lawyer then sent the debtor an information subpoena and written interrogatories that required him to answer a list of questions about the $1,809.54 debt. No answer.

December 9 was the last day of the 30-day time period. At the lawyer's request, the process server carried out a "nonmilitary" check to confirm that the debtor was not then a member of the armed services. Were that the case, he would not have been subject to civil court. But the process server reported that the debtor was indeed a civilian. Since he had not responded within 30 days, the lawyer prepared and submitted to the court a default judgment. Again he mailed an information subpoena and written interrogatories to the debtor. This time, the man refused to accept them.

The lawyer retaliated with a subpoena to take deposition of the debtor, meaning that under oath, the man would be forced to describe his assets and admit their location. Then, the plaintiff's attorney could legally seize them. Naturally, the debtor evaded personal service and required service by substitution. He also failed to respond to the subpoenas.

In mid-February, the lawyer obtained a court order that demanded that the debtor appear before a judge to "show cause" why he should not be punished for contempt for disregarding previous subpoenas served. (Sound familiar? Clearly, a devotee of the Powell School of Evasion.) The lawyer then served a restraining notice on the debtor's bank, preventing him from transferring or withdrawing money until he had paid the jeweler's judgment. The checking account was overdrawn; his savings account had only $6.

Meanwhile, the process server had been trying to

serve the show cause order requiring the defendant to appear personally in court. But the process server couldn't do so within the 30-day period specified by the court's rules, so the lawyer had to apply for a new order. Soon granted, the new order demanded the defendant's appearance in court on April 19. This time, the process server managed to serve the new order upon the debtor, but on April 19, the jeweler and her lawyer were alone in court.

On April 20, the lawyer applied to the court for a bailable attachment, which would empower his client to take the debtor's material assets to satisfy the $1,809.54 debt. After the attachment order was granted, the lawyer immediately wrote to the defendant, advised him of the latest action and requested a reply. No answer.

Hoping that the defendant would be cowed by a uniformed officer's appearance on his doorstep, the lawyer dispatched a sheriff to serve the attachment order. A few days later, the sheriff returned to the lawyer and said that the defendant had been so evasive and abusive that he had not been able to execute the bailable attachment.

Before the lawyer could act again, he was jarred by a call from the state attorney general's office. "We've received a complaint that you've been harassing a young man in Manhattan," said one of the assistant AGs in an icy tone.

Complaining about an attorney to the bar association or to the state attorney general is an old trick, usually intended to pry the lawyer from his or her case. Though the jeweler's young lawyer had done no wrong, he was concerned. He knew that being right was not always enough to avoid problems. A permanent file concerning the complaint had been opened and a further investigation, the assistant AG warned, would begin immediately. (After studying the case for a day, however, the attorney general's office dropped it.)

Two weeks in May slipped by. The lawyer and his hapless client sat to reevaluate the case. In eight months the attorney had spent $142 in telephone calls and filing fees, and his legal bill had grown to $1,000. The lawyer suggested the case be discontinued since the cost of the suit had already exceeded its value. The jeweler hoped to meet the defendant in court. No doubt the judge would direct the cheater to pay the judgment at once or return the watch. But who can wait that long? White had had enough.

Who is to blame for her misfortune? All the characters in this case performed according to the legal system's standard choreography. The jeweler's attorney fought with every affordable legal tactic until pursuit was no longer viable. The judges to whom he appealed granted the legal muscle he requested. But the legal system was not strong enough to quickly corner someone who was unwilling to submit to its authority. The jeweler didn't expect instant results, but she did believe that the system—in a reasonable amount of time—would recognize her loss, force the man to repay her the cost of the watch and punish him. Instead, the cheater used the court system to cheat her again by using time against her.

Over the years, I've seen dozens of cases where these kinds of evasive, time-consuming tactics were used by ordinary citizens, not just the high-level players like Adam Clayton Powell. As Powell so deftly demonstrated years ago, the legal system often favors those who *resist* their legal obligations, rather than those who shoulder them. You may sue someone to force him to meet his obligations, but by understanding the workings of the legal system, he can easily contrive a safe legal refuge.

There have been many high-level reports critical of the nation's court system. One landmark judicial report, issued while *James v. Powell* was running its tortuous course, was by the National Commission on the Causes and Prevention of Violence, which urged drastic revisions of the "fragmented, inadequate and archaic American machinery of justice."

A special committee headed by trial attorney Edward Bennett Williams (yes, one of Powell's lawyers) called for an overhaul of the criminal justice system, citing overloaded and understaffed courts, plea bargaining that had replaced traditional legal processes and intolerable delays that made Constitutional guarantees mythical.

Many of these problems persist today. But the legal crisis is not just in the criminal system; it pervades the civil system as well. In fact, while millions of both criminal and civil cases are filed annually in state courts, there are four times as many civil cases as criminal cases filed in the federal court system each year. So why is there no outrage—no call for a national commission examining the crisis in *civil* justice?

In fact, there have been a number of notable conferences and academic papers over the years, going back to the 1906 speech delivered by distinguished legal scholar Roscoe Pound before the American Bar Association, titled, "The Causes of Popular Dissatisfaction with the Administration of Justice." Perhaps the problem is that we have become accustomed to living with crisis: We are fed a steady diet of crises in the news media, which fuel and focus public attention—but not for long. Each "hot-button" issue seems to ignite and accelerate to a flash point, then give way to the "Next Big Thing."

But if we block out the crisis in timely civil justice, then we misunderstand the seriousness of situation. Exploiting ambiguity and endless procedural devices in the administrative law, a lawyer can heap enough motions and appeals upon the bench to choke the system with delay. The evasive defendant need not be powerful or rich; any man or woman can mount such a defense and succeed. Indeed, the strategies of defiance, whether open or subtle, have proved so successful against the legal system that today they are not the exception, but rather the rule.

Because business must somehow go on—despite the failings of the court system—we are dangerously encouraging our citizenry to go outside the law for solutions. And people like the jewelry store "thief" learn quickly. Because he has avoided serious punishment, the system did not teach him to behave differently in future disputes. More important, the rebuffed victim is not likely to remain rebuffed long. Thus, the system destroys its public support by punishing honest citizens and rewarding cheaters. The court's daily lesson now comes into sharp focus: Modern "justice" comes most often to those who can afford capable lawyers; have plenty of time; and therefore can exploit the system where it is most vulnerable—in its unwieldy administration, which dashes any hope of quick resolution. This is how trust, the judicial system's principal foundation, is destroyed.

This is the lesson Esther James is about to learn.

* * *

Time Fixes

*** Enforce court decisions**

Many people are dissuaded from taking their cases to court not only because of the time it takes to arrive at a decision but also because of the time it takes to *enforce* a decision—even if they win. A judge's order does not guarantee compliance, as Adam Clayton Powell demonstrated with obstreperous ease. The verdict against Powell should have ensured his payment; instead, it merely marked the start of another chase.

If we are to renew respect for the legal system, we must ensure timely enforcement of judicial decisions as part of the overall process. After trial or after the final appeal is settled, one of three actions must follow: 1) If the defendant has been found liable, he must completely comply with the judgment; 2) he must partially and regularly comply, based on his income; or 3) he must petition or be petitioned to the court for a declaration of bankruptcy. Any substantial lapse quickly destroys respect for the courts.

Clearly, the legal system is not powerful enough to wring payment from a truly defiant litigant. We might solve the problem by simply giving judges the enforcement power they lack, but this solution could be harsh and dangerous, saddling us with an authoritarian judiciary. Besides, our judiciary could never be made so powerful that a defendant today could not quickly bury his or her assets after trial to avoid payment.

Our objective is not to punish people for nonpayment, but to ensure payment. So we should pursue prosecution only after making efforts to prevent evasion. "Those who seek equity must practice equity," as the maxim goes.

One solution is to require both the plaintiff and the defendant to submit financial statements to the judge *before* entering the courtroom. To prevent later avoidance, each party would be required to file copies of three previous federal income tax returns and a description of the value and location of his or her assets, much as a bank requests when an application for a loan is made. After the commencement of the lawsuit, plaintiff and defendant could move their property only with approval of the court.

Neither party would have access to the other's records until (and unless) the plaintiff won. If, however, the defendant is judgment proof (that is, if he has no money or property), the plaintiff would be advised so he could decide to abandon the case. Alternatively, he may resolve to follow through, to push the defendant into bankruptcy.

The access to such records under the supervision of the court may pinch nerves of privacy, but how private is this information now? Numerous tax agencies have our personal accounts on file; so do a string of credit organizations, credit card companies and banks. Is there a substantial difference between their access and a court's access to this information?

Thus, by eliminating the legal hunt for a litigant's assets, we can save substantial time and judicial effort. Inevitably, some defendants will secretly shelter their property; that risk is inescapable. But at least under this system simple fraud can be easily proved. Serious discrepancy between actuality and the records filed under oath with the court would be conclusive proof of *criminal* fraud and an indictment could follow immediately. Ultimately, much of the legal footwork that Adam Clayton Powell taught us could be avoided.

*** Require litigants to attend their trials**

Today, few litigants go to court with their lawyers on their cases, not just because the law is so confusing, but because often the parties don't want to be inconvenienced. Yet it is their case; they are the ones involved and they should be exposed to its risks and frustrations *directly and personally.*

The legal process, often a mysterious operation monopolized by lawyers and judges, would become more comprehensible to litigants who were required to sit through months of courtroom tactics and maneuvering. The noxious effect of delays on everyone would be too obvious for most to ignore; and for most, that realization alone would discourage further tactics.

The courts were meant for ordinary people, not just for professionals. The trial is only a formal procedure for settling arguments. Since the plaintiff and defendant are at the center of the argument, what sense does it make that the litigants only understand half of what's going on? Ordinary citizens in court must always comprehend exactly what is going on, and they must be required to attend at all stages of the suit.

But understanding is not enough. Plaintiff and defendant must be made to feel that *justice* is in their hands, too, not just in those of the professionals. Only then will courtroom justice really mean something.

11

Powell: Disorder in the Courts

It's January 1, 1964. Nearly four years have passed since Powell made his televised "bag woman" charge. Eight months have passed since he was convicted of defaming Esther James in State Supreme Court.

The defamation decision now sits before a higher court, the Appellate Division. The ruling on Powell's contempt of court citation is wending its own circuitous way there.

James has not seen a penny of her award.

Four days after the citation for Powell's contempt is issued, he wangles a conditional stay of the State Supreme Court's order that he appear January 6. Meanwhile, Rubin and Covington will compose an agreement that will compel Powell to reveal his assets within 15 days after his appeal against the defamation judgment—if the court rules against him. The agreement also will ensure that Powell does not transfer any of these assets until the appeal, scheduled for January 24, is concluded. Finally, the congressman will have to sign and abide by the agreement by January 3.

This understanding is conceived in the chambers of Justice Charles D. Breitel of New York's Appellate Division. Powell endorses the documents outside his home in San Juan on January 3, and the agreement is signed by Breitel in New York soon after. With the judge's signature it becomes a court order that supersedes Powell's congressional immunity. But the question is, will Powell comply? And who can force him to do so?

On February 6, the Appellate Division presents its review of Powell's trial. The five appellate judges agree with the jurors that Powell did indeed defame James's character, but they reduce the damages award from $211,500 to only $46,500. The money is sliced from the punitive damages; the $11,500 compensatory damages award is affirmed.

Now Esther James and Ray Rubin have some decisions to make. If they do not like the reduced award, James could request another trial. A new jury could either affirm the Appellate Division's judgment or dispense a new version of justice—perhaps one more to her liking. Rubin sympathizes with his economic partner, James. She was "greatly disappointed" in having $165,000 cut from the award, he says, but she wasn't sure what to do. If she accepts the pruned award, Powell will have 15 days either to pay or to display his assets. The January 3 agreement will still stand even if the case makes its way up to the Court of Appeals.

Powell is on the floor of the House when the Appellate Division's decision is announced. William C. Chance, yet another Powell lawyer, says the reduced figure is still very high. He will advise his client to appeal *that* decision to the New York Court of Appeals.

On March 9, James accepts the $165,000 reduction. Powell is unavailable for comment—he is traveling in Spain.

Several days later, *NBC White Paper* presents a

lively profile of the congressman. Chet Huntley, the TV show's host, presents Adam Clayton Powell in all the roles he plays so well: a passionate pastor enchanting his flock; a hero to the oppressed (even while reclining in his lavish Puerto Rican home); a deft politician artfully deflecting criticism with humor; a black leader decrying white meddling in the movement for civil rights; an intuitive showman thriving on controversial publicity.

Indeed, while Powell's heaven remains in Harlem, his hell has broken loose in the courts. On March 1, State Supreme Court Justice Frederick Backen orders Powell back to court in May to account for his ability to pay the reduced $46,500 he owes Esther James.

Also on March 1, the court orders Powell's second wife, Yvette, to appear on April 3 to explain why she should not be cited for contempt of court for her failure to attend previous court dates set to discuss her husband's finances. She does not show on April 3 either; it's becoming a family tradition.

On April 8, James and Rubin launch another assault. They file suit in the State Supreme Court for $251,000 in damages and accuse Powell of transferring ownership of his Puerto Rican home to avoid paying the judgment. According to the James team, Powell transferred the home and property, worth $85,000, to his wife and to her aunt and uncle, Carmen and Gonzalo Diago. James names them all codefendants, along with Powell.

About a week later, a judge sitting in a local district court in Vega Baja, Puerto Rico, signs a warrant for Powell's arrest, based on charges that he fraudulently transferred ownership of his home to his wife and her relatives. This fraud case is criminal in nature—the one filed in New York the week before was a *civil* case.

The Puerto Rican court orders a hearing for May 20 and sets bail at $500. Powell, however, is not in Puerto Rico. Nor is he in New York on May 1 to submit to a financial examination in Supreme Court.

Justice Charles A. Loreto immediately orders Powell to report to the State Supreme Court on May 4 to explain why he should not be jailed for failing to hand over James's judgment.

Powell's attorneys, ever the artful dodgers, plead that Powell's examination should be postponed in consideration of both his congressional immunity and his duties on Capitol Hill. Request denied. Loreto rules that, because of the agreement Powell signed January 3, he can no longer claim immunity. Rubin then seeks an order for the King's arrest after he misses the examination on May 1. But this, too, is denied.

By May 3, 1964, 50 months after the fateful *Between the Lines* show, four of New York's courts are pondering various civil aspects of the case.

The State Supreme Court is trying to corral Powell on May 4 for a financial examination and some explanation.

The Appellate Division is to decide May 7 whether to stay the State Supreme Court's financial examination pending Powell's appeal of the defamation case to the State Court of Appeals.

The State Court of Appeals is wrestling with Powell's request that the judges overturn his original defamation conviction.

The State Supreme Court is considering a $250,000 damage suit against Powell.

Not surprisingly, Powell does not appear in the State Supreme Court on May 4. Justice Thomas C. Chimera tells Covington that by May 6 he has to prepare a defense for Powell's charges of contempt. The justice says he would consider later in the day, despite Covington's strenuous objections, whether to issue an order for Powell's arrest. Covington pleads with Chimera for more time to answer "the proposed drastic action."

In a highly unusual exchange, Chimera assures Rubin that Powell would sooner or later be "brought to book." The justice complains that he was tired of "a lot of ducking," but he also rebukes Rubin when the attorney requests that an arrest order be issued for Powell on the spot.

"What kind of justice would that be," the judge asks, "to issue an order without giving your opponent time to answer?"

Rubin suggests that if Chimera granted the arrest order, he might have Powell before the bench immediately.

"You're kidding," replies the judge. "As soon as I signed it the word would be out and you'd never find him."

The evasions, the arrogance, the paperwork, the frustration—it's all wearing on every judge who touches the expanding case.

Each time a judge hears a case, he must review the law and all past judicial decisions relevant to the plaintiff's and defendant's pending arguments. In cases such as Powell's, the jurist also must study the case's particular history, including its spin-off cases and all decisions attached to them. Four years of litigation have generated numerous motions, appeals, appearances in court and official decisions on all levels of the state's legal system—and a stack of paperwork eight feet high.

The case has been derailed by a defiant litigant whom the judges can do little to control. In an effort to avoid possible grounds for appeal, they can only proceed with agonizing caution, stalled at each step by technical obstacles requiring more research and judicial scrutiny. The judges are fast becoming fed up. Their remarks are veering out of line.

Of Powell's 20-year career in Congress, Justice Chimera once remarked, "I understand he doesn't spend too much time in the chamber." Covington hotly protested the judge's comment, pointing out that President Lyndon Johnson called Powell "the most productive chairman in Congress."

"I wouldn't be surprised if he did," replied a caustic Chimera. "He is also running for office." (One can only imagine what Judge Judy might say today!)

After the explosive May 6 hearing, Chimera postpones his decision on the order for Powell's arrest. He wants to "find some things out." First, was the House of Representatives really in session on May 1 when Powell was to have appeared in court? It wasn't, the judge discovers.

On June 1, Chimera orders Powell's arrest for civil contempt of court. Earlier, the judge had criticized the congressman's behavior as "so flagrantly contemptuous of the authority and dignity of this court as to promote a tragic disrespect for the judicial process as a whole. No man should be allowed to continue in this fashion and it is time for the defendant to answer for it." Powell, in Washington, D.C., breezily calls Chimera's ruling a great victory. "Now I can continue with my work," he says.

As long as the House is in session, all its members are immune from civil arrest. The lawmakers are slated to adjourn for several days, starting July 13, for the Republican National Convention, and then reconvene and presumably follow a similar schedule of adjournment for the Democratic National Convention starting August 24. Conceivably, then, Powell could be safe from arrest until the end of August. Chimera acknowledges that he cannot deny the congressman immunity during the session, whether he is "busy with important committee work or basking in the sunshine of Puerto Rico on any given day."

The justice also criticizes Powell's disregard for the January 3 agreement in which he waived his immunity. Long after Powell had endorsed and Judge Breitel had cosigned the agreement, Powell submits an affidavit in which he declares that "[he] did not contemplate that this agreement would bind [him] if it constituted 'a gross violation of [his] duties in Congress.'" To that, Chimera retorts: "[Powell's] blind assertion that he neither intended nor contemplated that his 'word' would bind him to the performance of such an act is a contemptuous acknowledgement that he never intended to keep his word from the beginning."

12

Time Troubles: The Problem with Contracts

I regret to find that the law was powerless to enforce the most elementary principles of commercial morality.
—Lord Herschell, in the case of Reddaway v. Banham, 1896

Linda Boreman was born in the Bronx, the daughter of a New York City cop and a strict mother. She attended various Catholic schools, and by the time she was in her mid-teens, her classmates dubbed Linda "Miss Holy Holy" because she kept her dates at a distance.

But Boreman also developed a deep ambivalence toward authority. She mistrusted strong authority figures; at the same time she was drawn to brutal and controlling men. In her early 20s, she began performing in hardcore porn films and found herself catapulted to the national stage as the star—known by her stage name, Linda Lovelace—of the 1972 film *Deep Throat.*

Deep Throat was one of the first pornographic films to feature plot, character development and relatively high production standards. It earned mainstream attention (despite being banned in large areas of the U.S.) and became the subject of several obscenity trials.

Produced for less than $50,000, the film became the most financially successful porn movie ever made. Most estimates put revenues in excess of $100 million.

But when I met with Linda Lovelace in the late 1970s to talk about a book contract for her autobiography, she was bitter and broke. She claimed that the $1,250 she was paid for her appearance in *Deep Throat* was taken by her violent and abusive ex-husband; she was suspicious of being exploited yet one more time.

Lovelace wrote the book *Ordeal* with one of my clients, the well-known newspaper columnist and author, Mike McGrady. McGrady's old friend and gadfly publisher Lyle Stuart agreed to produce the book and we hammered out a unique deal.

It was clear that we were dealing with a person of great notoriety, and that once word of the book got out, a lot of people would get very nervous. This book was being billed as a definitive look at the pornography trade in the United States, one that would show the exploitation, the violence and the double standard applied to women, who were forever condemned while men got a free pass. And it would name names—celebrities like *Playboy*'s Hugh Hefner and Sammy Davis, Jr.—in compromising roles. It was believed that many would take offense and go on the offensive, taking legal action to stop the book's publication.

Lyle Stuart agreed that once the manuscript was published, he would defend Linda against all lawsuits and pay her legal fees and any judgments in full if she or he lost the suits—all without interrupting her royalty payments. And if she had to sue for any monies due her, she could add the legal fees incurred in doing so to the monies she was entitled to receive.

Stuart took a calculated risk that people like Hefner would not sue. He was right, but other lawsuits were brought and as agreed upon, he defended them. The book became the stake Linda needed to start again: buy a house, settle in as a Long Island suburban housewife—and even become active in the feminist anti-pornography movement. If this had been the usual deal, Lovelace would have received little or no benefits from the book contract. The litigation that ensued was long, bitter and expensive, requiring traveling to other states and testifying in lengthy depositions.

While the key provisions of the contract focused on litigation, the underlying issue was—once again—time. The very existence of litigation interrupts the flow of any agreement, and the length of such suits ends up forcing people to make settlements out of court. So by guaranteeing Lovelace complete payment and requiring the publisher to defend her against lawsuits, we removed the issues of time and compromise, as well as her having to go through yet another ordeal.

Nevertheless, all kinds of traditional contracts, oral or written, have become increasingly meaningless when measured against the time required to enforce them. In the case of Adam Clayton Powell, for example, it did not matter whether or not he actually intended that his "word" would bind him to agreed-upon actions; any oral "contract" with the court became irrelevant when it could not be enforced in a timely manner.

Historically, a contract has come to represent the culmination of a negotiating process between two parties. Each party agrees to certain benefits and obligations, and the contract expresses them. While many contracts may be expressed orally—with a handshake agreement—our widespread preference for a written agreement affirms its importance as an accurate record of the details of a negotiation. It ensures against future discrepancies in memory.

But the demise of the contract has become evident across many businesses. "There's been a new definition of what a contract is," lamented an economist employed by an automotive products manufacturer in a *Wall Street Journal* article several years ago. "A price isn't necessarily fixed just because it's specified in the contract." Faced with an unexpected rise in prices, suppliers default on their agreements with wholesalers. Most of those contracts are routinely "renegotiated" since paying a modest price increase is often cheaper than paying the cost of a lawsuit. Besides, the company awaiting compliance also has schedules to meet; it needs the other's products *now*, not after years of legal wrangling. Complains an officer of a midwestern power company: "A contract used to be a contract. Now it's another stage in the negotiations."

These types of agreements do afford some protection in today's unpredictable legal system. Indeed, as written contracts have evolved with technology—from handwritten sheets to computer-generated documents revised endlessly over the Internet—it's not unusual for agreements to run 50 to 100 pages, with exhibits totaling thousands of pages. But even as contracts have grown progressively more complex, their increased bulk and detail have made them more vulnerable to legal defiance, not less. Each added provision contributes only more fuel for evasive argument and more opportunity for alternate interpretation, in effect, reducing the contract's legal strength.

And as Adam Clayton Powell so aptly demonstrated, time is the key: When we can't rely on a contract or agreement being carried out in a predicable time frame, then justice cannot be served.

Take the case of Eleanor Webster, whom I met several years ago when she was working part-time for Sail Realtors on Long Island. She took the job to make some extra money and help ease the financial pressure on her husband. After three months, she closed her first deal;

her commission was $7,000. Contracts were signed and exchanged. Several busy weeks slipped by and everything seemed to be going well. A closing date was set.

But a week before the scheduled closing, Webster learned that the date was reset, without her knowledge, for the next day. When she insisted on being there, Webster was told not to attend, but was assured by the seller that she would get her commission. She called her realty firm's lawyer, who explained that she had no case until the sale was completed. If her payment was withheld, she could take action; until then, she had only her suspicions that something was wrong.

The buyer and seller met the next morning and completed the sale. Within a couple of days the seller was on his way to a new home in Arizona. Webster's suspicions were confirmed—she had no commission. While it wasn't clear who was to blame, it didn't matter; there was no way to recover her loss in any cost-effective way.

* * *

Time Fix

*** Expand small claims court**

The small claims court system can help many ordinary citizens who need help in a hurry. Many legal experts have written about the effectiveness of small claims court, where legal jargon is often set aside and where lawyers are not often found. The jurisdiction of this court must be expanded, providing entry for cases with value up to $25,000; its method of handling cases, without formality and with common sense, is what the people need and want. The parties should be encouraged to represent themselves and the procedures of the court should be explained and simplified to accomplish this end.

Lawyers need not be indispensable to every action seeking justice. The role lawyers play in our judicial system might be diminished in some respects, but it's high time we put our human resources to better use. There's no evidence to support the notion that reducing the employment of lawyers would result in a system of justice that is less protective of our rights.

That said, we must be careful to distinguish the quick results delivered by small claims courts from the justice achieved *after* a decision is rendered. *Consumer Reports* has warned that "the Small Claims Court's machinery for enforcing a judgment—usually with a Writ of Execution against the defendant's property, his bank account, or his wages—is not always effective."

Streamlining the procedures of justice to save time is part of our challenge. But part of creating more efficiency in the system is also strengthening its credibility—repairing the average citizen's perception of the judge, the lawyers representing both parties, their debates in court and the power and authority of the court itself.

13

Powell: Appeals, Affidavits, Arrest Warrants—Oh, My!

By May 10, 1964, more than four years after Esther James was slandered by Adam Clayton Powell, her lawsuit has swollen like a bad bee sting:

(1) The original case, now a year after the trial verdict, has been submitted to the New York Court of Appeals, which is trying to decide whether the lower court had lawfully judged Powell.

(2) The judges in the lower Appellate Division are pondering Powell's motion to adjourn his ordered appearance before State Supreme Court Justice Chimera on May 1. It's already more than a week past that date, but the decision will still be important for Powell. If the judges rule in his favor, he will be pardoned for his failure to appear, and the order for his arrest will be invalidated.

(3) The appellate judges are puzzling over Powell's appeal of State Supreme Court Justice Markewich's contempt-of-court citation issued December 27. Should it be upheld or overturned?

(4) Four other actions—two civil and two criminal—preoccupy the judiciary. One civil suit sitting in State Supreme Court is for damages resulting from Powell's alleged fraudulent transfer of his house and property in Puerto Rico. Another civil suit in Westchester County, New York, is for damages resulting from Powell's alleged transfer of other property to avoid paying James's judgment.

Two criminal suits, potentially more dangerous to Powell than the civil cases, simmer over these alleged fraudulent asset transfers—one transfer in Puerto Rico on April 17, 1964, the other in Manhattan on August 21, 1963.

In Puerto Rico, a hearing is set for May 20 to force Powell's answer to charges that he fraudulently transferred his property in Cerrogardo to a relative. From Judge Angel Rivera Valentín in Vega Baja's Supreme Court comes another order for Powell's arrest. The judge sets bail at $2,000. But Vega Baja's police do not attempt to arrest the congressman, relaxing in his eight-room split-level home, 17 miles from San Juan.

Judge Rivera and Virgilio Mendex, Powell's attorney in Puerto Rico, agree that Powell will attend a hearing May 22, so he needn't be arrested. Now playing the role of a fair-minded litigant who merely tested the law and lost, Powell declares he is ready for reconciliation. "Legally James is right," he tells a reporter, "so there is nothing more I can do.... I think nobody wants to go to trial."

A brilliant performance.

On the day of the hearing, Powell dutifully reports to Vega Baja police headquarters. He chats for ten minutes with José Pérez Rodríguez, a district judge of Río Piedras, and then leaves. "We reached an agreement under which a trial will be held at some later date," Powell reports. One of the congressman's attorneys later says he understood that when his client presented himself to the police the warrant had been recalled. The judge and Powell apparently agree that Puerto Rican authorities will not attempt to execute the order until Powell's appeals are concluded.

Meanwhile, in New York, Rubin continues to pursue Powell's assets, trying to satisfy the original defamation judgment. Progress is slow until he receives a phone call from a woman who charges that during the past year Powell had siphoned $30,000 from Abyssinian Baptist Church funds for his personal interests. During that time, Powell had supposedly refused further regular salary; from then on he was to be reimbursed only for his "travel and business expenses."

Pouncing on this new clue, Rubin subpoenas the church's financial records from March 7, 1960, the day after Powell appears on *Between the Lines*. The church's attorneys object, asserting that because the church is not a defendant in the suit, its finances should not be revealed to James. On May 21, they move before State Supreme Court Justice Hyman Korn to quash the subpoena. At first, Korn reserves decision, but five days later he sides with Rubin, rejects the motion and orders the church's bank to present the record.

A month and a half later, while Powell is away at an international labor conference, the pending criminal suit in Manhattan explodes. On July 8, Justice Evelyn Richman of the Manhattan Criminal Court issues a warrant for Powell's arrest, citing Powell for "fraudulent conveyance of property"—that is, hindering, delaying or transferring funds to avoid paying a creditor. Under New York's Penal Law, this act is a criminal misdemeanor, punishable by up to a year in jail.

Rubin has accused Powell of transferring a $900 check to his wife, Yvette, when the congressman learned that Rubin intended to seize it to satisfy James's judgment.

The $900 was Powell's fee for writing a 1963 article in *Esquire* magazine titled "The Duties and Responsibilities of a Congressman in the United States." (No kidding.) Rubin charges that Powell asked his literary agent, Bertha Klausner, to supply a corporate check for payment to his wife, who in turn endorsed it over Powell's signature.

The charge is similar to the suits Powell faced in Westchester and Puerto Rico. All allege that the congressman had concealed or transferred his assets to avoid paying James's judgment. But this new criminal charge is Powell's only *immediate* threat, since he has negotiated the recall of the criminal warrant in Puerto Rico. Until the issuance of the Manhattan criminal warrant, Powell has been protected as long as Congress was in session—about ten months of the year—because of his constitutional immunity from civil arrest. During the other two months he simply has had to limit his visits to New York to Sundays, when he needs to preach before his congregation.

But this new action cannot be so easily sidestepped. Because the warrant comes from a criminal court, Powell will be vulnerable to arrest in New York on *any day*, whether or not Congress is in session. (The Supreme Court had ruled 56 years earlier that the Constitution guarantees all members of the House and Senate immunity from arrest "in all cases except treason, felony and breach of the peace," and this "excepts from the operation of the privilege all criminal offenses.")

At the same time, Richman cripples her own order for Powell's arrest with two stipulations: First, she suspends the warrant entirely until the New York Court of Appeals decides Powell's latest appeal of the defamation case. Next, she obliterates the Supreme Court's distinction between criminal and civil warrants by permitting the warrant's execution *only while Congress is not in session.*

On July 10, the Court of Appeals releases its decision on Powell's original conviction: It affirms the conviction and $46,500 judgment. But Powell is still safe at least until October 3, when Congress is scheduled to adjourn for the year.

Saturday, September 19, 1964, is Adam Clayton Powell Day in New York City. The Man, himself, rides down Seventh Avenue in a black Caddy convertible, leading a parade of 60 cars and four brass bands. Alternately holding clenched fists over his head and saluting the crowd, the pastor draws waves of cheers. Powell declares that he will not allow the Haryou Act—expected to bring millions of dollars into Harlem to fight juvenile delinquency—to founder in Washington. He will tolerate no "political shenanigans."

A champion of the oppressed, Powell points to 32 laws that have sprung from his House Education and Labor Committee. "My friends," he booms, "this is my record. But I am not content! I shall continue to fight until every single one of us is able to live a full life in the 'Great Society!'"

Harlem flocks to his call in November, although he runs virtually no campaign for his reelection. Of more than 100,000 votes cast in his district, Powell garners over 84 percent.

Naturally, Powell wants to join his constituents at the polls on November 3; he files a motion for special immunity from arrest for the day. Federal Court Judge Thomas F. Murphy turns him down. Two deputy sheriffs, armed with warrants for his arrest, wait in Harlem for his appearance on Election Day.

Powell also requests that the criminal arrest warrant issued by Manhattan Supreme Court Justice Richman be enjoined until his appeal of the court's decision has been reviewed by a higher court. Again, Murphy disappoints him.

Powell has appealed to the federal court to discard as unconstitutional Justice Chimera's State Supreme Court order directing Powell's arrest and confinement until he paid James's award. The Constitution, Powell insists, forbids the incarceration of a congressman over a civil dispute. But Murphy rules against Powell, holding that state authorities would have to decide the matter without the federal court's interference.

Powell's team appeals that decision, but on November 20, the U. S. Court of Appeals refuses to stay the civil arrest warrant. Powell's attorney counters, requesting that the court stay the issuance of the criminal warrant. The court refuses.

Powell's superstar defense attorney, Edward Bennett Williams, eventually pushes the question to the U. S. Supreme Court, asking its jurists to stay the warrant. Because the Manhattan Criminal Court failed to examine any witnesses in the case under oath, the lawyer argues, it lacks the authority to order Powell's arrest. But on Christmas Eve, Supreme Court Justice John M. Harlan, without any comment, denies Powell's request.

Meanwhile, in the criminal case involving Powell's $900 *Esquire* magazine fee, the congressman's literary agent, Klausner, swears in an affidavit that, excluding Powell and his present wife, she alone "would have any personal knowledge of all the facts and circumstances relating to or in connection with the conveyance alleged in the complaint [that is, Powell's arranging for the $900 check's payment in his wife's name to avoid paying any of James's judgment]." Then she also declares, "I have never given any testimony or have been examined in said criminal proceeding by a judge." Not surprisingly, the criminal court responds by calling Klausner in to discuss the whole affair on November 30—the same day Powell is scheduled to appear for arraignment. Neither she nor Powell (of course) elects to attend.

Justice Alfred J. Cause is predictably nettled when neither Powell nor his agent appears in his criminal court. The judge continues the July 8 arrest order against Powell. (No legal action is ever undertaken against Klausner.)

Williams visits the civil wing of the same court that afternoon and asks Justice Arthur G. Klein to prevent the criminal court from prosecuting Powell. Klein decides to take some time to consider the request and asks the district attorney's office to delay its pursuit until he reaches a decision. Several days later Klein denies Williams's request.

Powell immediately appeals that decision to the Appellate Division. Although he has not won permanent protection from both payment and prosecution with his appeals, he has always at least gained precious time—time during which his lawyers could search for more stalling technicalities as Rubin's expenses are multiplying.

On December 8, Justice Breital of the Appellate Division orders that the warrant will remain in place until Powell's lawyers, the district attorney and the state attorney general all submit briefs arguing the law in question.

Powell then returns to the State Supreme Court to force the warrant's reexamination, but he is threatened with a third citation for contempt of court. Powell has accrued $292.93 in court costs while unsuccessfully appealing the original conviction for defamation to the State Court of Appeals. Justice Edward T. McCaffrey wants that bill paid, so the justice orders him to show cause why he should not be cited for contempt.

As 1964 comes to a close, State Supreme Court Justice Samuel M. Gold announces to the court, "We are dealing with a person who has repeatedly flouted the orders of the court and shown utter contempt for them."

Then he turns to Powell's attorney, Edward Bennett Williams, with this caustic suggestion: Why don't you advise your client to pay the judgment and "come back to the salubrious climate of New York which he represents...and enjoy the blessings of New York full-time?"

Rubin reports that Powell has paid the court costs, plus interest, by money order. Still, the justice is unsure whether to punish Powell for contempt of court for previously failing to pay the bill. "Wouldn't justice be limping," Gold asks, "if he were permitted to come in at the last minute, throw the money on the table, say 'Here it is' and have the court do nothing about it?"

Gold is determined not to let Powell escape. For "evasive tactics" he adds $150 to the Congressman's tab. Powell hasn't paid any of the $46,500 but in a flippant gesture, he pays Rubin the added $150 in four money orders: three for $50 and a fourth for 40 cents, the interest, bringing Rubin's total collection thus far to $454.39.

Almost five years after Powell slandered James, and 21 months after his conviction for defaming her character, Powell's defense is still strong, and the stack of paperwork is now nine feet high.

So far, 54 judges serving several courts have considered various parts of this case—many of them more than once. The case is costing the taxpayers thousands of dollars and thousands of hours of court time.

Powell lives within a barricade of legal protection—eight attorneys have debuted so far. At one point, a besieged judge diverges momentarily from a proceeding and asks one of Powell's lawyers if he is being paid. Yes, the defender replies. (It is later reported that most were not paid their full fees.)

Each avenue of Powell's appeal seems blocked by the courts, but the King will not soon relent—especially since the U. S. Supreme Court is now reviewing the entire defamation case. One court had ordered him to pay James $211,000; the next court reduced the amount to $46,500. He will push the case along to any court that will let him present an argument. Perhaps his adversary would eventually abandon the chase—or agree to a compromised arrangement.

Anyway, Powell is in no immediate danger. Orders for his arrest have been issued three times, but none has resulted in his arrest; he is being careful to stay out of New York and Puerto Rico.

If the U.S. Supreme Court rules against Powell, surely his defense will become much more difficult. The reduced judgment of $46,500, now up to $51,000 with 6 percent annual interest, will hang indefinitely over his head. At least on this issue he will be able to contrive no more appeals, and because a defamation judgment is an *intentional* tort, it cannot be dodged by declaring bankruptcy. This debt will stand until paid.

But Powell understands that as long as he plays the debtor role, he will be in control; time will be on his side. He even tells Rubin on one occasion: "I will be old and senile and you will be a senior citizen before you see a dime of this case."

14

Time Troubles: Delay and Denial

Wrong must not win by technicalities.
—Aeschylus, The Eumenides, *485 B.C.*

In the early 1990s, I was co-counsel in a landmark pro football case that brought parties from all over the country to Federal District Court in Minneapolis. For both players and owners this suit was, well, a game-changer.

The complaint alleged that the National Football League's Plan B free agency system had a substantially harmful effect on competition for players' services, thus violating antitrust laws. The case involved the Players' Association from Washington, D.C.; the National Football League, based in New York; and eight players, including the lead claimant from Long Island, Freeman McNeil, an All-Pro running back for the New York Jets and the namesake in the suit.

Why did we file suit in Minnesota, when none of the parties were based there?

Not surprisingly, time played a major role. Compared to venues in other states, the Minnesota federal court had a relatively short calendar that enabled us to get to trial relatively quickly. The case could have taken two or three times as long if brought in a more congested federal court.

In an unusual twist, I was also called as an expert witness in the case, testifying on the rights of contracting parties who rendered "unique services" and the valuation of those services. Over the years, I had negotiated contracts for many talented, high-profile clients, including McNeil.

Still, I found myself surprised at the emotion and stress I felt as I testified that the league's system was onerous and made it difficult for players to seek proper compensation. This was a big-league case, involving outstanding lawyers on both sides who were adroit at every nuance of prosecuting and defending a case.

At one pivotal moment an attorney asked me: "Isn't it true, Mr. Curto, that negotiation is a two-way street?"

"Yes," I said. "The problem is, there are six lanes going in one direction and only one in the other."

When we finished—the case took three years, including a trial that lasted several months—I was mentally spent. But we won, and the victory was followed by a players' class action suit that eventually led to today's free agency/salary cap system in the NFL. Five years later, Boomer Esiason, the former pro quarterback and now a network TV and radio color commentator, would note that McNeil "paved the way for a lot of players. He put his reputation, his name and his face on the line."

If not for McNeil, many players would have been denied just compensation—and if not for our decision to try the case in Minnesota, that denial might have been magnified by years of delay in other court systems.

Today, delays distort the quality of justice in many ways. The uncertainty of any case's outcome is exacerbated by the evolution of "truth" between the first summons and the trial—often months and sometime years later, long after any decision can deliver meaningful justice.

Consider the predicament of one of my former clients, Janet Larienel, an unmarried woman who had gotten pregnant some years ago. She had gone to her lover—her boss—soon after she knew of her pregnancy, and told him she wanted their child and asked for his financial help. He refused. If she wanted a child, that was her business. He would finance an abortion, but nothing more.

Larienel approached a partner in my firm in an effort to force the child's father to assume his share of the support expenses. In response to the lawyer's questions, she described her boss's fleeting visits to her apartment, his generosity and her naïve acceptance. A "strong case," the attorney called it. At first, she felt relieved. After all, the child was half his responsibility and he could easily pay his share. The lawyer predicted almost certain success, with some luck, within the year—unless the case was appealed. But Larienel could not wait a year. A decision several months in the future was worthless, since she could not risk losing the case at a point when she could no longer obtain a safe, legal abortion. She had already decided that she could not meet the expenses of raising the child alone, so she felt she had only one choice. She aborted the child.

The legal system failed Janet Larienel. The courts simply could not move fast enough to define her rights, to provide her the option she felt she deserved: raising her own child.

This case took place in the mid-1980s, but for many people today, the amount of time consumed in litigation remains the critical issue. If each side's witnesses are sworn to describe their recollections of events that took place in the distant past, little of their testimony is likely to resemble the truth. The truth has long been buried in lawyers' rehearsals.

Witnesses whose memories are "refreshed" by counsel will "remember" vividly the events of a long-gone day—though they could scarcely recollect the events of a day of last month. Thoroughly tutored in their legal rights and obligations, they carefully tailor their stories to fit the law and serve their own interests. And often, by omission, they deliberately distort the facts to gain a legal advantage.

Opposing claims, exaggerated to anticipate inevitable offers of compromise, may actually *appear* true through the prism of time today. After so long, who can truly tell what really happened?

Adam Clayton Powell maneuvered brilliantly through the legal system, launching appeal after appeal, adroitly avoiding arrest, but he owed much of his protection to the structure of the legal system itself, which allows for innumerable time lags and delays.

Knowing the system's vulnerability to people's fleeting memories, lawyers today try every tactic for delay, every theatrical stunt, every psychological ploy—irrespective of its relevance to the case. And the more delay between the event that initiated the case and the court date, the more likely that what takes place has little to do with what actually happened. Thus, the court becomes a mock stage.

Time also distorts justice in more indirect ways. With delays of often years, witnesses frequently disappear. Like anyone else, they may be transferred by their employer, simply move or die. As time passes, witnesses may lose sight of the importance of a case and no longer consider their appearance in court worth the effort and expense of returning to testify.

For the defendant, during the delay he may similarly occupy a house or apartment, drive an automobile, or sail a yacht. He may refuse to deliver a product that he is using, reselling or holding in inventory. While the lawsuit endures, he can benefit from the property of the plaintiff...for years. And each time the plaintiff advances, the legal system will tirelessly defend the cheater by confounding itself with technical dodges and by burying litigants, their attorneys and witnesses and all the facts of the case in a cascade of paper.

At a time when people commonly live in one state and work in another, obstructive litigants can further confound the legal system merely by doing business in states where they do not reside. Suppose, for example, the importer of ballpoint pens breaches a contract to deliver a shipment of pens from France to a store in New York City. The store owner, who has partially paid for the pens, lives in Connecticut. The importer lives in Wheeling, West Virginia, but his business is legally located in nearby Pittsburgh, Pennsylvania. Where should the case be tried? Let's assume the store owner is able to obtain a judgment against the importer and chase down his assets from state to state. In each state, legal proceedings would have to be conducted by an attorney licensed in that state. One lawyer would not suffice—multiple lawyers and added fees would be needed.

A trial probably would not begin for several years, and even after the case ground to "conclusion," the defendant could simply cart his assets into yet another state. The agonizing process would continue, and to the plaintiff, compromise would sound like wonderful relief.

With delay, business opportunities are missed; the value of disputed property is often lost; much hardship, pain and expense are often suffered unnecessarily. The eventual translation of these losses into monetary judgments after years of delay rings only vaguely of justice. Money is not a substitute for lost property and lost opportunity. It can neither restore lost years nor erase the anguish most suffer while awaiting a case's conclusion. Pretending that human problems can ultimately be solved after years of delay by showering them with money only dilutes popular respect for the system. It merely disguises the system's inability to produce timely justice.

Given the opportunity to tell the truth in court, most people would do so. Most lawyers also would like to speak directly to the real issues of their cases. Most witnesses would rather genuinely recall an incident in dispute than star in a rehearsed stage production. And most judges would rather dispense real instead of contrived justice. To give truth a chance, we must not allow it to be hijacked by time.

* * *

Time Fixes

*** Settle jurisdictional disputes up front**

The fragmented structure of our courts virtually ensures jurisdictional problems when a case involves an interstate dispute. Different courts simultaneously claim or refuse jurisdiction over the same case, issuing conflicting rulings, causing endless confusion, appeals and thus delays. Furthermore, the system's vulnerability to jurisdictional argument invites outright defiance from litigants.

As we have seen in *James v. Powell*, Adam Clayton Powell's attorneys often challenged a presiding court's right to rule on certain issues, insisting that jurisdiction belonged in some other court.

Still, the legal questions generated by jurisdictional debate are usually clear; each court's jurisdiction is prescribed by statute. Courts must have authority over both the property and the people involved in the issue in order to bring about its resolution.

These questions are often vital to a case's outcome. Skilled attorneys, recognizing a case's jurisdictional defect, may deliberately proceed with the case—only to upset its "conclusion" late by proving the court never had authority to hear it. In such instances, all the time and energy expended by the plaintiff in lower courts have been wasted.

The importance of jurisdiction cannot be diminished, but the mechanism for settling jurisdictional disputes has to be accelerated. Verifying a court's jurisdiction must not be so delayed that the decision comes long *after* the court, presuming appropriate jurisdiction, has settled the issues of the case. The question of jurisdiction over the subject of the case must be noted in a timely manner and then segregated immediately from the parent case. A decision must be rendered promptly, its appeal heard and settled soon after. Such a procedure would affirm the court's authority to hear the case and thus eliminate another form of uncivil disobedience.

*** Codify monetary awards**

As we have seen in the Powell-James case, the battle over monetary awards often prolongs litigation for years, adding huge amounts of time (and money) to the cases themselves.

These awards generally fall into two categories: compensatory damages to offset the victim's expenses and earning power; and damages for considerations such as "pain and suffering"or punitive damages for malicious behavior (such as Powell's defamation case).

In an accident case, for example, compensatory damages offset a victim's expenses and loss in earning power resulting from the crash, while pain and suffering awards supposedly compensate the victim for the pain and suffering he experiences because of the accident.

The compensatory award, which commonly amounts to several thousand dollars, is a calculated figure: How much does the plaintiff stand to lose as a result of the accident? Medical bills and an automobile's repair are added to produce part of the award. But what about the damaged ability to earn money at one's old job? That figure is a bit more elusive.

Suppose the victim is bedridden for months or years, or without a job for several years, or forced to abandon his career entirely because of the injury. How long must the defendant support the plaintiff for his negligence?

The court usually estimates what the victim would have earned had he or she not been injured; it tends to assume that the plaintiff will not find another career. But suppose the person does find another job? Should the defendant then continue to pay? In most cases, he has already paid the judgment in full by the time the plaintiff gets another job.

While compensatory awards often vary dramatically (and unacceptably) from case to case, the awards for pain and suffering or punitive damages can be truly unpredictable, shocking and disconnected from reality.

Certainly money helps the plaintiff to stop complaining and genuinely feel better. But how exactly does money compensate plaintiffs for the pain and suffering they endured as a result of an injury? Exactly what is the intent behind these gigantic awards?

The philosophy hinges upon the magic of money. Money provides a distraction from one's injuries; it attempts to give the victim a sense of satisfaction that the misfortune dealt him has been balanced by the court's award, and also that the defendant has paid for his negligence.

But who should pay for pain and suffering? In these cases, the intent of such awards is supposedly to "make the victim whole," not to hurt the defendant. Yet the current arrangement seems more like punishment than restitution—revenge is often the spirit in which jurors, impassioned by an expert lawyer, award colossal judgments.

Since automobiles account for the vast majority of negligence cases, and since most states require their drivers to be insured, it is the defendant's insurance company that usually pays the legal tab. And what that means, of course, is that *we*, the public, end up paying, since bills for pain and suffering are passed along to the rest of us.

In recent years, our legal system has assumed responsibility for permanently righting the wrongs of life. The hundreds of thousands—even millions—of dollars given to plaintiffs are not meant to ease their adjustment to an altered lifestyle. They are meant to restore life to as-it-would-have-been by creating "happiness" with money to counterbalance pain and suffering. This is not a realistic goal for our legal system.

Payments for pain and suffering must be handled through a modification of the Workers' Compensation program, with a basic monetary award assigned to every conceivable physical injury. Then, to account for differences between cases, after hearing all testimony, the judge or jury could ascribe a multiplier (say, one to three times) to the base award for each, including compensatory damages, and add this to the damages for pain and suffering.

Even in other cases, such as Powell's defamation suit, where punitive damages are awarded to punish malicious behavior, jurors and judges could be given maximum and minimum amounts within which they can place their awards. Whatever the specific guidelines, we must restrain emotional judges and jurors to reasonable judgment, or in their well-meant desire to issue justice, they will further damage the credibility of the courts. And we must do this on the spot, at the time the case is tried, not after appeal.

15

Powell: The Supreme Test—and Beyond

Almost five years after Powell's interview on Channel 13, the courts finally dispose of the original defamation case. On January 17, 1965, Chief Justice Earl Warren's Supreme Court, without comment, refuses to hear Powell's case. Powell's team had argued that the New York Court of Appeals had violated his freedom of speech as a congressman and private citizen. By refusing to hear the case, they eliminate Powell's defense once and for all. The next day, Edward Bennett Williams, Powell's attorney, announces: "We have reached a dead end."

Yet, when asked whether Powell would now pay James's judgment, the attorney hedges. Powell himself would make that decision, the lawyer says.

Excuse me?

The highest court in the land has essentially directed Powell to pay Esther James's judgment but the final decision is Powell's? Indeed, Powell long ago learned the impotency of the system. Far from fulfilling his sentence, he is contemplating disregarding the High Court.

For Esther James, on the other hand, life is hard. She is already serving a sentence of seclusion in her Harlem apartment. She buried her husband, a Pullman porter, in 1952; her children are all married. These days, five burnished locks line her door, like dials on a vault. Her telephone number is unpublished. To contact her, her lawyer calls, lets the phone ring twice, hangs up—to signal his identity—and then calls again.

On October 20, 1964, James earned even more notoriety on a relatively rare excursion from her apartment. She became a key witness in a case involving a hoodlum who walked up behind a small-time gambler standing about three doors away from her apartment and fired a bullet into his brain.

New York District Attorney Frank Hogan, whose office handled the case, has also been eyeing the Powell case for some time. After Powell misses his arraignment in November, a member of Hogan's staff announces that the DA is considering seeking "criminal information" from a grand jury—that is, asking a grand jury to investigate whether there were grounds to prosecute Powell criminally. The most important consequence of such a development will be to replace James as the damaged party with the district attorney and the State of New York—substantially strengthening the legal effort to settle the civil case.

Furthermore, with the grand jury's vote of criminal information, Powell will lose his present immunity from criminal arrest. He could be arrested in certain states and shipped back to his home district.

But even an extradition action will not be simple. New York has extradition agreements with many, but not with all, states, and not with the District of Columbia, where Powell will likely reside during the session. The King can avoid arrest by simply staying out of those states sharing an extradition pact with New York.

Shortly after the Supreme Court upends Powell's case, word leaks from the district attorney's office that Hogan will soon join the chase after Powell if James's judgment is not quickly paid. A week later, a grand jury begins its scrutiny of Powell's affairs, searching for evidence of suspected fraudulent transfer of funds.

The grand jury is armed with a power never before granted a non-congressional body, giving it special permission to review Powell's financial records archived in the system of private congressional accounts. Powell files a motion to block Hogan's access to the files; Hogan fires back countermotions. Powell plays the race card: "Instead of trying to determine whether a crime has been committed," he says, "this all-white grand jury had been trying to make up a charge out of whole cloth....If a black Congressman can be harassed and exposed to the uncertain vagaries of politically inspired justice simply because of the color of his skin, millions of black people all over this democracy are just that much more insecure."

The battle rages for 16 months.

After questioning more than 20 witnesses and thoroughly dissecting Powell's financial records, the exhausted grand jury cannot vote an indictment of criminal information against the congressman. Hogan's pursuit fails.

While Hogan draws Powell's fire, James launches yet another attack: She sues him again for $250,000, accusing him of transferring his property in Puerto Rico to evade the judgment. This civil suit had sprung from the criminal case still smoldering in Puerto Rico. Trial is set for February 11 in State Supreme Court.

When the process server attempts to serve Powell the summons and complaint, the congressman refuses to accept them. This evasion reduces the February 11 session to a jury inquest. Instead of deciding whether Powell is liable or not, the court will presume his liability and consider only how much he should pay in damages. After hearing all testimony, the jury presents a stunning verdict: Powell and his wife should be forced to pay $100,000 to James in compensatory damages, and Powell alone should pay $250,000 in punitive damages.

His wife resides full-time in Puerto Rico, though she earns $20,578 annually on the federal payroll. (She complained of not receiving her checks reportedly intercepted in Washington by her husband.)

The opinion of the judiciary, however, is decidedly different. State Supreme Court Justice Frederick Backer scolds Powell's peers for their "totally excessive" judgment and summarily reduces the reimbursement and punishment to a total of $210,000 (including James's original award). After adding the interest of $5,500, which had accrued on her outstanding $46,500 judgment, the total now stands at $215,500. James paces the corridor adjoining the State Supreme Court courtroom. "You know," she says, "at the outset I'd have been satisfied if the congressman had gone on the air and made a public apology."

In this case, as in Powell's first conviction, the jurors attacked Powell far too vigorously to suit his crime. They were enraged by the bold mockery of justice, frustrated by his genuine political power and insulted by his brazen disrespect for the public.

Between 1965 and 1966, Powell makes 65 well-publicized trips to Miami and Puerto Rico with his staff at the taxpayer's expense. He weekly preaches to his congregation that they have a "divine right" to break the law "until they have a share in making the law."

He is routinely accompanied on his official business trips and in the news media's eye by comely and clinging young women—his "secretaries" and "special consultants"—though he is a married Baptist minister. In the spring of 1965, asked about his active interest in women and high living, he admits: "I like my wine and my women."

"His behavioral traits and longtime abuse of power are well-known to the American people," says Florida Republican lawmaker Sam Gibbons. "Citizens from all walks of life want corrective action."

Congress also is aching for a chance to discipline Powell. He had ascended to a position of great legitimate power in the House and from that perch, he continually embarrasses and insults his colleagues.

He takes full credit for the anti-poverty bill; claims that he invented the domestic Peace Corps before Sergeant Shriver thought of it; and boasts on television in February that his committee "controls 40 percent of the legislation of this nation."

He accuses John Williams of Delaware, who led the fight in Congress against Powell in 1963, of attacking him "because I am Negro." He rationalizes his spending of the public's money in European nightclubs by describing Congress as "filled with men and women who are doing the same things....Equality is equality....I'm a member of Congress as good as everyone else. I will always do what every other congressman has done, is doing and will do."

Rubin is determined to turn Powell's political strength into vulnerability. In a letter dated March 9, 1965, James asks United States Attorney General Katzenbach to start a *quo warranto* proceeding to question Powell's eligibility to hold office. The congressman, she outlines in her request, was not in New York from October 3 to December 3, 1964, including the day of his most recent election to the House. Therefore, he should not be considered a resident of his own district, as the Constitution demands, and should be expelled from Congress.

On March 15, Rubin is in federal court complaining that Attorney General Katzenbach has ignored his client's request. Judge John Cannella obligingly signs an order directing the attorney general to show cause the following Tuesday why he should not institute such proceedings. On April 30, another federal judge, Charles H. Tenny, then decides the court has no jurisdiction to force the attorney general's action and dismisses Rubin's case. James's lawyer fails in this skirmish, but his new strategy is correct: Powell's greatest vulnerability lies with his congressional colleagues' long desire to be rid of him.

Enjoying a congressman's protection from prosecution while speaking on the floor of the House, Powell again attacks James. He accuses her of being a "finger woman" in the killing she was said to have witnessed in October, secretly pointing out the victim to the murderer.

At the same time, however, he intimates that James would soon have her money—at least the $46,500 of the first judgment she won. Members and friends of his church have raised $6,000 and his political cronies in Washington, $10,000. He hopes to have enough by the end of April, he says, to pay the judgment. But he will not pay the additional $163,500 award—that decision he will challenge and defeat, he promises.

A month later, State Supreme Court Justice Charles A. Loreto begins to doubt that the $163,500 award can actually stand up to Powell's challenge, for technical reasons. The strength of the judgment depends entirely upon Powell's exact address in Manhattan. Rubin had thought Powell resided at 120 West 138th Street, but Williams, Powell's chief counsel, declares that his actual address is 2368 Seventh Avenue. Therefore, Powell's lawyers argue, the legal papers of the case have all been improperly served and are as flawed as the jury's verdict. Both will have to be discarded.

Loreto ponders the argument for several days, and finally settles on a compromise. He sets aside James's second award on the condition that Powell and his wife accept service of legal papers for a new trial. Furthermore, Powell must agree to pay Rubin $83.43 to cover the court costs of setting aside the $163,500 judgment.

With that last major obstacle set aside, Powell visits his home district on April 7, 1965, for his first weekly appearance in five months.

Before Judge Arthur Braun on the criminal court's bench, Powell and two attorneys answer the criminal arrest warrant issued in Powell's name for the fraudulent transfer of the $900 check. Powell has come to face the court, late or not, under his own power, his lawyers point out; an arrest warrant is clearly unnecessary. They ask Braun to parole Powell and to schedule a hearing for later that month. Assistant District Attorney Patrick J. Moynihan (who will later serve as U.S. senator from New York) then speaks up. "In view of the defendant's reputation," he says, he has no objections. Braun paroles Powell and warns him that if he jumps parole, the court will come after him again.

The hearing is subsequently postponed, and then adjourned because of the grand jury's investigation. When the grand jury eventually decides to vote "no bill" against Powell, the case is automatically struck from the criminal calendar. Powell has returned to his city "to get this thing out of my hair....I talked to friends in Washington. They urged me to get it over with. It's been bothering me. I've got so much work in Washington....I'm handling practically the whole domestic program of the nation."

The next Sunday, April 11, Powell returns to his congregation with a thundering sermon entitled "The

Imperishable Dream." "Great God...great big pious God...omnipotent God," he roars, his chasuble hanging from his outstretched arms like a huge pair of wings. "Thank you!...Thank you God....You safely brought me home!...Great God, what a day! What a day of victory!"

Later that month Powell announces that his friends have raised about $30,000 of the $52,000 he needs to pay James's judgment. They had staged a round of social events, including a cocktail party at Billy Simpson's Ebony Table in Washington where Powell's supporters paid $50 per glass. The congressman says that if he doesn't find the rest within a few days, he will simply "borrow like LBJ" to get the rest. (President Johnson had said recently that he had borrowed money to pay his income tax.)

But by the end of April, Powell's tone abruptly changes. He says he will not pay the $52,000 unless all related civil suits are dropped against him. James and her counsel rebuff the demand.

Then the widow from Harlem gets a break. An anonymous caller tells Rubin that Powell's cronies have stashed all the money they have collected in the Freedom National Bank on West 125th Street in Manhattan. Rubin telephones the bank. Posing as another well-heeled buddy of Powell, he asks how he can contribute to the fund. "They told me to make out my check to 'Harlem Justice for Powell' and mail it to the bank," Rubin later says. He drives to the bank and drops a subpoena and restraining notice in the hands of bank president William R. Hudgins. The restraining notice seals the account; the subpoena instructs Hudgins to produce the account's records in State Supreme Court on May 20.

Hudgins never answers the subpoena. Instead, another bank official discloses that by mid-May the checking and savings accounts credited to the Harlem

Justice for Powell Committee contained $18,000. Two months later, State Supreme Court Justice Morris E. Spector orders the Freedom National Bank to hand over the money to James and Rubin to partially satisfy their judgment, which has grown, with interest, to $53,000.

Hudgins visits Raymond Rubin's office on August 2, 1965, and hands Rubin two certified checks totaling $19,115.54. Rubin gives James $11,000, and keeps the balance. Finally, their efforts have begun to pay off, but James and Rubin are far from breaking even on the case. The original jury had calculated that James would lose $11,500 in earning power because of Powell's defamation, but after waiting more than two years, she has not even won all of that compensation. Rubin isn't faring any better; he estimates that his expenses for prosecuting the case over the last five years amount to $20,400.

But they have gone too far to quit now.

16

Time Troubles: Unjust Alternatives

Litigation is a machine in which you go in as a pig and come out as a sausage.
—Ambrose Bierce, The Devil's Dictionary, *1911*

Some time ago, the owner of a soft drink company was faced with a deadbeat distributor who refused to pay his bill. Eventually, the frustrated owner turned the case over to me. I decided to bring a civil action in State Supreme Court to collect the bill of several thousand dollars. After almost two years of fighting, I was close to victory. I had secured a judgment against the distributorship and was about to make a levy—to seize his property in order to satisfy the judgment—when I got a frantic call from the distributor.

"I already paid it," the man cried.

"What do you mean you already paid it?" I said.

"I already paid it," he repeated. "These goons came to my house and said if I didn't pay, they were going to break my kneecaps—or worse. So I paid them."

I called my client to find out what was going on. He told me that at a party one evening he happened to mention to a friend the predicament he faced with this distributor. "Would you be happy with half?" the friend asked. "I'll take care of it." So the friend collected all of the money, kept half and gave the other half back to my client—who hadn't told me.

Apparently, the owner had given up on courtroom justice—it took too much time. He wanted his money *now*, so he pursued an alternative approach.

Over the years, as courtroom justice has become increasingly less timely, more and more people, like this soft drink company owner, have begun searching for alternative mechanisms. It's not that judges don't strive to make the system work. Indeed, over many years of tangling with Adam Clayton Powell, many judges involved in the case clearly wanted the legal system to work—they *believed* they could make it work. But Powell and his legal team showed them just how vulnerable the system had become. Even the judges were powerless in mandating timely justice when the system was manipulated by litigants intent on fomenting delay and defiance.

Trying to oversee cases shuffled from one court to another, judges are seen as the personification of an ineffective legal system. To litigants, judges often seem arbitrary, more interested in moving a case forward than in concluding it fairly. Judges complain about overloaded calendars, while regularly granting extensions to parties that may help avoid conflicts but further bog down the courts. Their legal deliberations and decisions seem irrelevant to the lay person because they *are* often unrelated to the real issues of the case.

The judge cannot control the substance of these debates. As rival attorneys contrive complex challenges and counter-challenges based upon technicalities, judges must laboriously consider and rule on each; otherwise, the case may be overruled by an appellate court. They frequently demand settlement to ease the congestion in the courts, but litigants aren't always privy to the judge's discussions, which usually take place in chambers and only with the parties' attorneys.

As a result, many frustrated litigants now attempt to force justice through strategies of public "shaming"—sometimes through exposure and punishments imposed by consumer protection agencies, other times through the embarrassment and humiliation meted out by the news media, especially high-profile TV and radio personalities, the "action" reporters. These approaches have matured into cheap, fast—but often undependable—alternatives to the courts.

The modern consumer protection movement, which began in the 1960s and 1970s, was initially supported by the broader civil rights movement. The cry went out: If you've been wronged, you can seek justice without wasting time (and money) in court. Some advocates chose to protect consumers through nonprofit watchdogs, while others turned to quasi-judicial government agencies.

In the "preventive" wing of the movement, some groups such as the Consumer Federation of America have lobbied for legislation to provide consumers with information to identify fraud and dangerous products. Other watchdog organizations infiltrate supermarkets, department stores and factories; they test the calibration of scales; examine shelved merchandise; verify its labeling and confirm that only approved ingredients are used in manufacturing.

Government agencies at various levels also respond to consumers' pleas for help when they feel wronged. These advocates have powerful administrative weapons: fines and subpoenas; the authority to issue regulations for businesses within their jurisdiction; the authority to issue and revoke licenses. But one of the most pervasive forms of "public justice" has evolved under the glare of broadcast news media scrutiny; the aim often is to embarrass "bad" companies or individuals before millions of consumers.

The first prominent example of this kind of program was *Call for Action*, which debuted in 1963 on New York's WMCA radio station. Judging by the public's enthusiastic response, program founder Ellen Strauss immediately was "convinced that the service had to act as an advocate for all the people who were powerless to help themselves," wrote Frances Cerra in the *New York Times* a year later. The program's strategy was to accept calls from listeners who could not get results from the courts.

Eventually, Strauss's *Call for Action* model was refined, packaged and transplanted across the country. Scores of newspapers and radio and television stations established "hotlines" as part of the consumer crusade. After receiving a complaint, most would send a form letter to the alleged offending company notifying it that a consumer had complained and that the station was on their trail. Would the company resolve this matter? Usually, it would comply quickly, but to counter occasional defiance, the station would report the incident in print or on prime-time TV, with a derisive wag of the finger: "Shame on you!"

One of the most successful pioneers in consumer advocacy was Betty Furness. After running New York State's Consumer Protection Board and serving as New York City's Commissioner of Consumer Affairs, Furness joined WNBC-TV New York in 1974 to launch *Action 4*.

Within 16 months, Furness won more than $300,000 for her complainants, taking on corporate giants such as Macy's, BankAmericard and Kaufman Carpets. In less than two years, her staff of eight was "resolving" about a thousand complaints a week. The potency of her strategy, Furness said, was simply explained: "Nothing in the world has the impact of TV—that's where the people are."

Indeed, Americans often have turned to the media—not only print and television, but increasingly the Internet—for solutions to life's problems. But "justice" dispensed through the media can be risky and unpredictable. What happens, for example, when a reporter makes a charge against a corporation, particularly one that's a sponsor of his TV station or an advertiser in his newspaper? While news executives usually stand behind veteran reporters, there's no question that big advertisers can apply pressure on the media in an effort to curb negative publicity—sometimes in direct actions like costly lawsuits.

Programs related to the consumer's plight remain popular not because the public believes that justice must be done, but because they get high ratings—and high ratings attract advertisers. The public likes to rally around a spirited counterattack against the "ruthless" corporation that has fleeced the ordinary guy. "They litigate by public feeling," observed one former Federal Trade Commission official.

The "action reporter" model has remained popular in the news media partly because it appears to offer consumers a shortcut through the bureaucracy of the courts—the costs, delays and frustrations of litigation—and a way to get action. But just how effective is it these days? At a time when the media landscape is undergoing explosive changes—fragmenting into myriad cable and satellite channels and Internet sites—public embarrassment at the hands of an action reporter no longer has the impact it used to have. The public is easily distracted in 24/7 news cycles, and subjects of media reports are better prepared to respond and rebut—or simply ignore—such scrutiny.

Even the so-called victories proclaimed by consumer agencies do not promote justice. In fact, they represent a step backward. By dispensing justice through government agencies—including investigations, the determination of guilt and imposition of penalties—we only further undermine American justice and disguise our legal system's failure. Consumer protection agencies end up changing places with corporations, making them plaintiffs instead of defendants when they try to reverse a summary judgment—and awarding consumers an enormous legal advantage, fair or not.

Because a consumer agency's ombudsmen are almost always political appointees, they are also likely to be sensitive to pressures from various quarters, inside and outside government. When a mayor, for example, decides that a well-publicized attack on certain business practices would improve the city's image, a consumer agency could be particularly tough on the offenders—until a new priority target is declared at City Hall. Or when a crowd of angry citizens rally at the state capitol, or in Washington, D.C., calling for immediate consumer protection, government agencies can bypass the lengthy legal process by handing out fines and lifting licenses. They get results in a hurry for the public, and thus may be valuable political tools. But in the process, many honest as well as unsavory operators may be punished. At best, these agencies provide results, not necessarily justice.

Many businesses, in turn, have retaliated with their own alternate forms of justice, such as retaining collection agencies to get restitution from unscrupulous customers or clients. Collection agents appear at the accused debtor's place of business, demanding repayment in front of his fellow workers and superiors. And they appear at his home, repeating the tirade. They telephone at odd hours and angrily demand "our money."

All these alternative justice vehicles derive their power from fear: fear of public embarrassment; fear of consequent financial loss; fear of the loss of a good credit rating. And the rationale for all these approaches: They get results.

Of course, there also have been some "kinder, gentler" alternative approaches to litigation, notably Alternative Dispute Resolution, or ADR. Sometimes called the "quiet revolution," the ADR movement uses processes such as mediation and arbitration to resolve or avoid conflicts. ADR programs have been instituted by government agencies as well as a growing number of companies and industries. One of the most important initiatives in the movement came through the 1990 Civil Justice Reform Act, which enabled dozens of federal district courts to try out court-annexed ADR programs. The court-annexed ADR programs have resulted in high satisfaction ratings, and certainly, the movement has been an attractive alternative to many organizations seeking to circumvent unacceptably high litigation costs.

But critics point out that even court-annexed ADR settlements do not create legal precedents and offer the public limited transparency of the judicial process. Real justice can be broadly served only from well-run courts, an advocacy system in which the parties argue their position in a timely fashion before an impartial jury and judge with rights of appeal. While a consumer agency may be perfectly capable of investigating cases of consumer fraud, its hearing room is not a legitimate courtroom nor is its commissioner a true judge.

To get justice, consumers should not have to telephone or write to an action specialist in the news media; recruit pickets to parade at a store's entrance; or appeal to the consumer affairs department. They simply should be able to go to court.

* * *

Time Fix

*** Keep the same judges on a case**

All cases are born of human disputes and all are best solved with direct, personal discussion. Confronting a different judge at each legal appearance impersonalizes all judges. Judges must be seen as a *people*, not anonymous mannequins in black robes; they should not appear remote; they belong *in* the case.

Litigants working with the same judge each time they come to court would less likely feel lost in an impersonal legal maze. They would develop a feeling for his expectations. The whole process of justice would assume a warmer and more human tone; such continuity would benefit everyone in the courtroom.

Judges following each case from beginning to end would learn much about a litigant's motive. Deliberate stalling—much more difficult to pull off in person than on paper, and particularly when facing the same judge at every session—would likely decrease. Judges would consider each question of law not as an unreal exercise related to people they have never seen before, but in the context of a real human dilemma. They could develop a sincere interest in each case's fair resolution, and litigants would surely sense the judge's heightened interest. And finally, there would be much less paperwork—and much less time wasted on painstaking analysis, passed from court to court.

17

Powell: A Cacophony of Contempt

By mid-1965, Powell has defaulted in yet another suit, the Westchester case in which James accused Powell of transferring half his interest in his house to his first wife, Hazel Scott, to prevent its seizure in order to offset James's judgment. He is scheduled to appear in State Supreme Court in August for a financial examination to determine his ability to pay $33,000 he still owes from the original judgment.

Powell does not appear. The court directs him to explain why he should not be cited for contempt of court for ignoring the order—even though Powell has already been cited for contempt once, and no one is quite sure whether he could be cited again for contempt in the same damages suit.

The cases staggers into November and Powell is again directed to appear in court to disclose his finances. This hearing is to preclude James's suit for $250,000 in damages filed in Manhattan for the allegedly fraudulent transfer of his home in Puerto Rico. Powell again does not comply. As before, he is ordered to show cause why he should not be cited for contempt of court. Powell has now ignored at least seven similar orders to appear on issues related to his failure to pay the original $46,500 award. He is imperturbable.

But on December 1, Powell's defense team suffers another setback. Presiding Justice Saul S. Streit of the New York Supreme Court demands to hear Powell's defense against the charge of the fraudulent transfer in Puerto Rico. "This man," the justice lashes out, "is not to be believed or trusted."

Two weeks later, State Supreme Court Justice Maurice Wahl decides to increase Powell's penalty. Recognizing that a defendant who indulges in a malicious fraud and deception to evade paying court-ordered penalties is liable for further civil punishment, Wahl orders Powell to pay an additional $575,000: $500,000 in punitive damages, and $75,000 in other compensation. The justice believes a term in jail would be better medicine for Powell, but that punishment is beyond his authority. His frustration, like that of his colleagues, surfaces unmistakably in court: "He's like a mackerel," the judge says, borrowing a 19th century quip from Senator John Randolph. "He shines but he smells to high heaven."

Such a remark could hardly have come from a dispassionate officer of the court. But in his desire to punish the congressman, Wahl unwittingly plays into Powell's strategy. His damage award is so high that it will surely be reduced drastically, if not overturned, by a higher court. The judge's position is clear: Angered at Powell's deft choreography around the system, Wahl wants to prevent him from further embarrassing the courts. But in lashing out, he ends up embarrassing the courts even more.

The congressman's friends strike back. On

December 17, the board of deacons at Powell's Abyssinian Baptist Church demand in a telegram to Presiding Justice Bernard Botein of the Appellate Division that Wahl be returned to the civil court where he regularly served.

The issue is no longer Powell's debt nor James's five-and-a-half years of hardship, but Powell's assault upon the system. He is lighting the way for countless others to follow. So far, Powell has defied the will of the court at almost every turn.

When James leaves the courtroom on December 14, 1965, she is elated. "I think the King is still dead," she tells reporters. She still doesn't get it.

For most of the next year, the legal battling over Powell's case focuses on the great game of contempt of court. This is a difficult and exhausting game; its rules are complex, vague and ambiguous. But it suits Powell's interests nicely, and he ends up playing that game with more finesse then anyone had before him.

The first rule of contempt is: Anyone who commits an offense against the court, such as refusing to obey a court order, can be cited for contempt of court.

Ah, but there are subtleties. The first is the crucial distinction between *civil* and *criminal* contempt. Civil contempt is basically one person's wrong committed against another while they are locked in a civil suit. This type of contempt is usually cited against a person who has failed to meet alimony payments—or, as in Powell's case, payments for defamation. When the payments go unpaid the harm is entirely private; only the person who is unpaid is affected.

Criminal contempt is usually imputed to one who offends a judge—and thus, the public, whom the judge represents. There are additional subtleties. The citation for criminal contempt can be issued under Judiciary Law—a civil statute—or under Penal Law. Contempt under Judiciary Law is not a crime; under Penal Law, it is.

Powell's defense dances to a score of legal conundrums. Could he be charged with criminal contempt in a civil case? If convicted of criminal contempt under the Judiciary Law, could he be arrested on Sunday in the state in which he was convicted? (Remember, Sunday is the day on which civil justice rests.)

On January 18, 1966, Powell's attorneys oppose Wahl's $575,000 damage award, arguing before the appellate judges that the State Supreme Court exceeded its authority when it added money damages to the original award. In a 3-2 decision, the Appellate Division disagrees, while conceding that the original award was much too high. They trim the judgment to $155,785, which includes the $33,000 Powell still owes in the original $46,000 award.

Rubin then mounts a barrage of contempt charges against Powell. In April the congressman is held in civil contempt for failing to give testimony on his financial condition. Action on this charge is still pending in July, when Rubin fires off three more charges of contempt. His strategy is simple: He has exhausted all civil remedies so punishment for criminal contempt is the only way to force Powell to pay. Under criminal contempt, an individual can be arrested anywhere in the country on complaints issued by proper state authorities. At the time, the maximum penalty is a fine of $250 and 30 days in jail.

The first of Rubin's requests for a contempt order is for Powell's failure to pay about $155,785. The second is for his neglecting to pay Rubin $581.70 for court costs on three of Powell's unsuccessful appeals. The third is for Powell's ignoring several court orders in the original defamation case.

Shockingly, on July 20, Powell actually appears in

State Supreme Court to answer the contempt charge grown out of his failure to pay the judgment or to explain why he has not paid it. He isn't worried about the state's eager sheriffs—with Congress in session, Powell could not be arrested under any outstanding warrant. Thus, with comforting impunity, he argues against Rubin's motion calling for the congressman's delivery to jail for 30 days. He complains that the legal papers have been improperly served and are thus invalid. Finally, he does dispose of one charge of criminal contempt by paying his overdue court costs of $581.70.

On July 28, after lengthy consideration, State Supreme Court Justice Irving H. Saypol attempts a compromise. He orders Powell to pay off his debt piecemeal, at a rate of $600 per week. Saypol also has been considering a motion to punish Powell for criminal contempt for not paying the judgment. But in the end he denies the motion for technical reasons: There is a typographical error in a court order, a recurrent nightmare for all lawyers in long and complex cases.

"The time has come," Saypol tells reporters on August 9, "to come to grips with the problem." He threatens Powell with a year in jail unless he appears in Saypol's court in three days for a financial examination and discussion about James's unpaid judgment.

Powell's three-day allowance is up. Saypol waits for Powell to appear as ordered, but the congressman decides he would rather spend the day fishing in the Bahamas. On August 12, a furious Saypol reverses his previous ruling on contempt under the Judiciary Law.

On September 1, Pastor Powell delivers a scalding sermon, criticizing President Johnson's administration for flouting the law—failing to coordinate antipoverty programs. A nice touch.

On September 14, Saypol orders Powell to stand trial before a jury for criminal contempt of court. The jury will decide on Powell's willfulness in violating five judicial requests, three subpoenas and two court orders.

Powell claims he is disturbed by the word "willfulness." He argues on September 26 that the State Supreme Court has no authority to hold a trial to decide such a question as Saypol's. The Appellate Division grants him a temporary respite, but shortly afterward the five justices unanimously agree that he should stand trial for contempt.

The judiciary begins to close in from another front: On October 3 State Supreme Court Justice Harry Frank declares Powell guilty of a third charge of civil contempt. This one stems from Powell's transfer of his house in Puerto Rico. Frank blasts him for "ignoring, evading or abusing legal procedures" in not paying the $131,000 he owes—the present punitive damages, plus interest. Frank orders Powell to court, but of course, the congressman does not comply, and on October 14, yet another civil order for Powell's arrest is issued by the court. But Congress is in session, rendering the order ineffective.

After five days, Powell's trial in State Supreme Court ends abruptly. The jury discusses the case for less than an hour and declares that Powell has indeed willfully violated five court orders and subpoenas to appear for his financial examination. Powell is not there to hear the jury's decision and neither are his attorneys. Four of them had arrived for the trial's opening, but only to contest the court's jurisdiction. Contrary to the appellate judge's opinion, they say, the State Supreme Court is not empowered to act on a case of criminal contempt. Therefore, they will not recognize its authority by participating. Together they rise, pack their attachés and troop out.

In their absence, the trial sails smoothly. The jury declares their verdict; Judge Matthew M. Levy affirms their decision.

Another skirmish in the Appellate Division ends on October 26, this time in Powell's favor. The justices rule 4-1 that the congressman cannot be cited for contempt for a sixth order he violated. The Appeals Court renders this decision after reversing a ruling by a State Supreme Court justice. In that court, the judge approves a motion to punish Powell criminally for ignoring a subpoena to pay Rubin $293.12 in outstanding court costs. "Failure to obey a subpoena [which is issued by a lawyer but not a judge] in civil proceedings is therefore a civil not a criminal contempt," the Appellate Court decides.

What does all of this really mean?

At the very least, it undermines the verdict for criminal contempt in Levy's State Supreme Court, based upon Powell's violation of three subpoenas and two court orders. The Appellate Division has not commented on contempt related to court orders, but Section 751 of the Judiciary Law might provide Powell a strong defense on that score. According to that section, when the criminal contempt is not "committed in the immediate view and presence of the court, the party charged must be notified of the accusation and have a reasonable time to make a defense."

Powell's defenders could still conceivably argue that their notice was not adequate, nor were they given sufficient time to prepare their case. The Court of Appeals had previously ruled that there could be no universal guidelines for sufficient notice and reasonable time. This could only be judged in the context of each case.

Nevertheless, the Appellate Division holds Powell in civil contempt and orders his appearance on Friday, November 3, for his incarceration for 30 days. If Powell comes to court he can be arrested under two other arrest orders. In other words, they are sentencing him to 30 days in jail. They must have known that he would not commit that blunder.

Williams, the congressman's chief counsel, admits his delight with the decision since by that time no one really knows the truth about the case. All that matters is what the courts say.

On November 4, State Supreme Court Justice Levy sentences Powell to 30 days in jail and fines him $500 for civil contempt of court. He has ordered Powell to court to present arguments over the punishment he would receive and to argue the effect of the Appellate Court's ruling on the case. On two separate occasions, Powell has indicated through counsel that he would appear in court. But on the date scheduled, Powell is nowhere to be found. The jail sentence—the fourth assessed to Powell—will be stayed for two weeks; the arrest order will be signed November 28.

Five of Powell's lawyers do come to State Supreme Court in their client's place. They vow to appeal Levy's decision to the Appellate Division. They will eventually lose, but that is unimportant. None of the arrest orders can be carried out outside of New York State.

On Election Day, Powell's constituency jams Harlem's polls, with almost three-quarters of them casting their ballots for him, thus ensuring his twelfth term in the House. Powell spends his birthday, November 29, vacationing with a beautiful young "house assistant" on Bimini, his sun-baked retreat in the Caribbean. There he can often be seen driving around the island in the old Checker cab he had imported from Washington to suit his fancy—and perhaps to remind him of the Capitol, which he seldom visited.

James has returned to her birthplace, Montego Bay, Jamaica, leaving her attorney alone in New York to fight the Powell gang.

18

Time Troubles: Compromising Positions

A lawsuit is like an ill-managed dispute, in which the first object is soon out of sight, and the parties end upon a matter wholly foreign to that on which they began.
—Edmund Burke, A Vindication of Natural Society, *1756*

In the mid-1960s, the Cold War between the U.S. and the former Soviet Union was still in a deep freeze. The great Russian dissident writer, Aleksandr Solzhenitsyn, was struggling to publish his work, which was quickly being restrained by the KGB. Solzhenitsyn had served years in work camps as a political prisoner; was freed from internal exile and exonerated; and became an international sensation with the publishing of *One Day in the Life of Ivan Denisovich*, which brought the Soviet system of prison labor to the attention of the West.

Thereafter, the KGB seized a number of Solzhenitsyn's papers, including the manuscript for his novel, *The First Circle,* which he had tried unsuccessfully to publish in the USSR. Frightened but determined, he continued working feverishly on his monumental work, the three-volume *Gulag Archipelago*. Under constant surveillance by the KGB, Solzhenitsyn worked on sections of the manuscript in the homes of several trusted friends—possession of the entire manuscript would have incurred the risk of a long prison sentence for "anti-Soviet activities."

Over the next few years, through the aid of a coterie of these friends, copies of *The First Circle* (a shortened version) and *Gulag* were smuggled out to representatives in the West and published with much acclaim. In 1970, Solzhenitsyn was awarded the Nobel Prize in literature.

I was among a small group of allies in the U.S., including the distinguished *New York Times* correspondent and editor Harrison Salisbury, who brought Solzhenitsyn's literary works before an intrigued public. But it was not an easy task, putting Solzhenitsyn's work into print—without putting him in a Siberian prison.

In order to constrain writers from shipping their manuscripts abroad, Russia at the time refused to sign the Berne Convention (established in Berne, Switzerland), a long-standing international agreement that protects the intellectual property rights of authors. While it was obvious that translations of Solzhenitsyn's novels had somehow leaked out of the Soviet Union, what protected him was that there was no written authorization in Solzhenitsyn's hand linking him to any of these translations or publications of his works. I created a legal theory that no work could have a copyright under the Berne Convention without some document in writing from the author. And since Solzhenitsyn had no contract with anybody, there was no evidence that he was behind any orchestrated effort to manufacture or distribute the translation of this manuscript abroad.

Instead, I created a trust in which the trustee was given Solzhenitsyn's work with the instruction to have it translated and published without disclosing the name of the person who gave us the manuscript. The trustee was then capable of filing for the trademark protection.

Using a trust provided a key advantage: When an individual creates a trust and delivers the corpus of the trust with instructions for the trustee to do something with it, those instructions are legally enforceable orally. This is one of the few areas where actions are enforceable without a written contract. So publishing deals involving hundreds of thousands of dollars were signed on Solzhenitsyn's behalf based on simple oral instructions, sometimes delivered through intermediaries.

When Solzhenitsyn came to the West (he was deported from the Soviet Union in 1974) his publisher and I continued to make settlements on his behalf, executing complex documents. This practice always gave Solzhenitsyn the insulation from face-to-face discussions and placed his representatives in the middle. Tax settlements and trustee accountings also were done in this manner. As a result, Solzhenitsyn often paid excessive taxes, but that didn't matter to him. Life in Russia had made him suspicious of all authority; he wanted no entanglements with the law. He put his trust in people, not contracts. Besides, his concern, above all, was that his books got published.

The Russian government never could marshal the evidence needed to prove he was guilty of any subversive crime related to the publication of his work. In the end, the trust, absent Solzhenitsyn's signature, protected all parties involved, although not without some compromises. By avoiding traditional legal processes, Solzhenitsyn sometimes put his friends in risky positions. But such compromises had another calculated, critical aim: They saved time.

In reality, *not* having written agreements with publishers in the West helped get the books out quickly.

And the quicker the books got out, the quicker they were widely publicized in the mainstream media—and the greater the level of protection he secured for himself and his collaborators.

Over the years, I've observed that many high-level clients, like Solzhenitsyn, seem more inclined to work out compromises than to risk outcomes of the legal system. The amount of time consumed by lawsuits has distorted our basic concept of justice, translating it into a financial value, as we would evaluate any common business venture. The plaintiff wonders: "How long will the case take? How good is the defendant's lawyer (and how good is mine)? Can we get him to compromise on a settlement?"

The defendant, meanwhile, calculates: "How long a battle can the plaintiff afford? How can I hold out against the courts? How many roadblocks can my attorney throw up? If the plaintiff gets close, will he be willing to settle? How much will my defense cost me, and how much do I stand to lose if I settle instead of holding on to a final judgment?"

These kinds of strategic calculations of cost-effectiveness have given rise to consulting firms whose main goal is to advise clients on litigation decisions. For example, one California-based firm, DecisionSet, conducted a study in 2008 where they found that most plaintiffs who decided to go to trial instead of accepting a settlement offer ended up getting less money than if they had taken the offer.

While the amount of litigation filed has increased over the years, the number of cases that are actually tried has decreased markedly. According to recent research, less than 1 percent of the cases filed in state and federal courts are actually resolved by completed litigation.

The trend in "vanishing trials" may reflect, in part,

a growing preference for earlier settlements through Alternative Dispute Resolution. But it also shows just how congested our court system has become. A civil suit today usually requires years just to reach trial, and with that kind of delay, it's not surprising how much pressure litigants feel to settle cases outside the courts. To get a good picture of our how ineffective our judicial system is, let's compare it to other institutions in our communities. What would happen if, say, 99 percent of the people who entered a doctor's office to be treated for an illness were forced to seek alternative treatment because the wait was too long? It would be intolerable.

Increasingly, judges have realized that without stern persuasion to force settlements on litigants, they cannot contend with their case loads. So the traditional process of administering justice has been perverted in order to maintain the flow of cases through the system. The judicial short-circuit—compromise—is now the cornerstone of American justice.

On the surface, employing compromise seems entirely reasonable. From childhood, we're taught that compromise is always better than conflict. From our history books, we recall famous political compromises, such as the gallant compromise of 1850 forged by Senator Henry Clay of Kentucky. When Congress exploded over the issue of slavery in 1849, the 72-year-old Clay, gaunt and tubercular, returned to the Capitol after a seven-year absence to deliver his impassioned plea: "A compromise scheme of settling amicably the whole question in all its bearings." Dubbed The Great Compromiser, he succeeded in forestalling the dreaded Civil War, if only for a few years.

Since Clay's time, we have seen many leaders achieve recognition as architects of compromise in highly charged and potentially bloody disputes. Each side has won a little, lost a little but ultimately agreed to some concessions to avoid risking the greater hardship of defeat.

With compromise so deeply entrenched in society at large, it's easy to see how it settled into the judicial system. It seems a natural extension of its role in settling international disputes. And since compromise is often a time-saver, it seems eminently practical to the judiciary.

But unlike international politics, the judicial process is strictly governed by substantive principles and procedural rules that set forth prescribed legal conduct, restoring rights and property to those deprived of them and punishing those who have unjustly benefited.

Diplomats may well compromise to solve complex questions between countries according to the conventions of international diplomacy. But as for domestic conflicts, our nation's law provides a discrete answer to every dispute. In criminal matters, a defendant is either innocent of the crime with which he is charged or guilty "beyond a reasonable doubt." Similarly, the litigants in a civil case are judged liable or not, according to the standard of a "fair preponderance of the evidence." Even a split decision of a jury or panel of judges provides resolution.

Fundamentally, the legal system is designed to produce judicial decisions, not shortcuts. At the same time, out-of-court settlements need not necessarily represent a subversion of our system. Were two litigants to settle their differences and freely withdraw their case before their scheduled day in court, even if after a judge's urging, the system may yet have served them well—so long as they had the recourse of promptly trying their case in court. When that practical legal recourse is denied because of calendar congestion, justice is no longer obtainable.

Such compromise is common in the "insurance game." Suppose, for example, you buy a new car and insure it against collision with your insurance company.

A few months later, you skid on icy pavement and crash into a stone wall. Luckily, you emerge uninjured, though the car is totaled. Figuring that the car is worth (after depreciation) about $27,000, you file an insurance claim for that amount. A few weeks later, you receive from the insurance company a check for $23,000. You immediately call the company for an explanation. The claims adjustor insists you are only entitled to $23,000, according to the company's Index of Depreciating Automobile Values. Satisfied?

No. You call your attorney and, together, you contemplate filing a lawsuit. "Look, I want to help you," your attorney advises, "but you can bet this case will take over a year to get to trial—maybe more. I've got to take a third of what we win; I can't afford to do it for less. If we win the full $27,000, I will take $9,000 and leave you with $18,000."

So the question becomes: Does the difference between the amount offered in settlement and the maximum amount you could win in a lawsuit justify the risk of the suit? The $27,000 will hardly cover the cost of renting or financing another car until the case is concluded. You might have to wait a year, and you will still be unable to replace your old car without adding more money to your final settlement. What you need is another car, *now*. But as insurance companies well know, immediate action is precisely what our legal system cannot provide.

Moreover, your attorney reminds you that there is no guarantee that you'll win the case for the full amount. Your most practical strategy is to hope that you and your insurance company can reach an out-of-court compromise over the $4,000 difference.

Such compromise may better serve your attorney's interests as well. Why? Remember, the lawyer has his own bills to pay: children in school, mortgage, taxes, overhead. To meet these obligations, the lawyer may rationalize that this is the best settlement he can get for his client, failing to acknowledge the warp in his own judgment.

The prospect of gaining resolution without shortcut compromise is even worse when you're fighting an insurance company over repair of your house badly damaged by a disaster like fire or flood. Say, the contractor and interior designer estimate your home's restoration will cost approximately $182,000. You quickly forward the estimates to your insurance company, but the company offers you $161,000. So you decide to go to court. But even if you're lucky enough to get a sympathetic judge who agrees that your case should be preferentially tried, you will probably find yourself counting weeks and months passing before any decision is rendered.

Where shall you shelter your family until then? Where will you get the money to pay the contractors and the decorators? Can you afford to rent a temporary residence as well as to pay to repair your damaged house...for a year or so? While the trial lasts, the insurance company will hold the full $182,000—or whatever you win—for the duration. Thus, by using the pressure of time against you, the legal system actually *encourages* the insurance company to deny the claim, litigate and resist settlement.

What path do we choose, then, to decide whether we should take our case to court or settle? How can we estimate the final recovery, the stakes we will have riding on the spinning wheel of American justice? We can know neither the odds nor the stakes; we can only gamble. Or we can abort the case and compromise outside the courtroom.

* * *

Time Fixes

*** Expand the role of magistrates**

Several alternatives have been proposed to commission alternative professionals to act as judges. One popular suggestion is to greatly expand the U.S. Magistrate Judge System, which was created in 1968 to help cut the judicial caseload. Already, thousands of these appointed lawyers assist federal district court judges by performing various duties, including serving as judges for the trials of civil cases when all parties consent; ruling on pretrial motions; conducting pretrial and discovery proceedings; and serving as special masters in civil cases.

This expansion is long overdue. Our judges have been suffering silently for too long. Perhaps they feel it would be undignified to confront the political authorities in making an urgent case for expansion. It wouldn't be the first time professionals have been restrained by their own image. It is time that lawmakers who have not appreciated the gravity of our judicial failure be compelled to act.

*** Broaden authority of judges**

Our judges must be freed to act quickly and without being unduly constrained by the possibility of appeals and reversals on trivial or irrelevant aspects of a case. Contrary to public perception, most cases are simple, and if a judge is authorized to limit the issues and direct the court's efforts to their resolution, the system will again become alive and responsive.

"Law is not just an idealized system of rules," noted New York Law University law professor Richard A. Epstein in the spring 2011 issue of *National Affairs*. "It also involves the public administration of those rules by a wide range of elected and appointed officials in an endless array of particular circumstances. For those who would defend a just legal order, the basic challenge is to strike a proper balance—between limiting the discretion of these officials so that they do not undermine the rule of law [and] allowing them enough leeway to perform their essential roles."

Like other public officials, judges must be empowered to perform their essential roles, in part by limiting the issues in a case and the amount of time spent in making oral and written arguments. A vigorous bench with broad powers to limit the time allotted to a case would unclog the system in a hurry—and enable litigants *not* to choose compromise over expedience.

Let judges have extensive pretrial discretion so they may get the case to trial quickly. Let the parties present their evidence quickly; let the judge from the bench move the process along, get the principal issue in dispute before the court in the shortest period of time possible—and end it.

If we speed up the system to complete a case in one year instead of five years, would we not use substantially less legal services? Less lawyer's time, less court time and less client's time. Benefits will naturally come from shortening the time it takes to get to trial. With less time between the start of a lawsuit and trial, there will be much less time for secondary issues. A day in court, not compromise, will become the norm.

19

Powell: Final Indignities

Powell's appeal of the Appellate Division's 30-day sentence lands before an unsympathetic Court of Appeals. On December 1, 1966, the Justices vote 6-1 to uphold the sentence. The next day, State Supreme Court Justice Joseph Brust desperately tries to reach another compromise. He orders Powell to pay $60 per week to James until he covers the entire debt of $164,000. Powell's attorney, Edward Bennett Williams, is understandably satisfied.

James's attorney, Raymond Rubin, is disgusted. At $60 per week the debt would actually grow over the years—and even if the interest were set aside, at the $60 rate, James would have to wait 53 years for the award to be paid in full. By then she would be *121 years old.*

Indeed, it was Rubin who had initially suggested a schedule of weekly payments, but after Brust's bizarre decision, he withdraws the motion and resumes the hunt for Powell's elusive assets.

A week later, Powell is scheduled to appear in court—he promised to do so if the Appeals Court ruled against him. The high court indeed ruled against him, but Powell is not about to leave Bimini for New York. He is passing the time drinking an exotic concoction of milk and Cutty Sark, playing dominoes, fishing and entertaining guests. His friends had organized a "Club 60" in New York—60 members who each would contribute a dollar a week toward his debt. Asked about his foes—including much of the judiciary, his legal adversaries and now many of his congressional colleagues—Powell says, "God bless them."

As the New Year is ushered in, the Court of Appeals is trying to decide whether to affirm the $131,000 that was added to the original monetary judgment when Powell was first held in contempt. The appellate judges are questioning whether Powell could be held for criminal contempt in a civil case. The three citations for civil contempt are in various stages of appeal.

By the end of the month, Powell's adversaries in the House close in on their iconoclastic colleague. The lawmakers had already voted to deprive him of his vote until a special subcommittee had presented their recommendation.

Powell calls a news conference on Bimini to announce that he will pay the $33,000 he still owes James on the original judgment rendered nearly four years ago. His lawyers, now including William Kunstler, the renowned defense lawyer, had advised him to do so. But Powell, as always, will not pay the full judgment. His strategy is to stall the courts until he can have the judgment reduced or arrange for somebody else to pay it. Friends in Washington. Friends in New York. Friends in the Abyssinian Baptist Church. Anonymous donors.

This time the payment, Powell says, will be financed from royalties advanced to him by Jubilee Records, which had pressed a record of Powell's choicest sermons. The record company executives expect to sell a million copies of the moving oratory, "Keep the Faith, Baby." Powell's share will be 22 cents per copy.

Wearing a sporty ensemble of blue shirt, blue shorts, blue socks and blue sneakers, Powell speaks out to his many enemies: "I'm going to pay based upon a poor humble parish priest's earnings, and I want to thank you all for making me eventually end up being a millionaire," he says. "I thank you for that. Just keep on hitting me. Keep on hitting me. Don't stop. Don't stop, please. Don't stop."

On January 31, 1967, Rubin at last receives $32,460 earned from Powell's album royalties. James's lawyer figures that Powell still owes about $3,700 in interest and miscellaneous fees, and two weeks later, Rubin receives another $3,447. Discounting $1,000 in court costs, he has thus far disbursed about $55,000 in pursuing the case against Powell—about $300,000 in today's dollars. His share to date is less than half; the balance of the money passed to James.

Meanwhile, Rubin clings to his strategy of trying to corner Powell with contempt citations. He tries a fifth and sixth time. Still, the anger and frustration pressing the judges caught between Rubin and Powell sharpen. State Supreme Court Justice Emilio Nuñez says that Rubin is technically correct in his latest maneuvers, but the judge nevertheless dismisses the lawyer's attempts: It "would amount to a Pyrrhic victory."

On March 1, the House of Representatives votes to disregard a subcommittee's modest recommendation for punishing Powell and excludes him completely from the 90th Congress. The following day, however, the Court of Appeals issues a ruling that reduces James's previous year-and-a-half of legal battling to a virtual waste of time. The justices vote 6-1 to excuse Powell from paying

$100,000 in punitive damages of the $155,785 judgment rendered by the Appellate Division. (Remember, the $155,785 award was a reduced version of the State Supreme Court's judgment of $575,000.)

The Court of Appeals declares that the congressman's behavior "was not so gross and wanton as to bring about the class of malfeasance for which punitive damages should be awarded." The court then stuns Rubin and James by unanimously deciding that the issue in the case involving $55,785 in compensatory damages must be returned to the State Supreme Court and retried according to Puerto Rican law, not New York law.

"Since the real property is located in Puerto Rico," the court rules, "the law of that jurisdiction—and not of New York—is controlling on the question of whether the conveyance made by the Powells was fraudulent and whether what they did gave rise to a cause of action for compensatory damages."

Powell is tanning in Bimini when he hears the court's decision. "Beautiful," he says.

A few weeks later, the Appellate Division affirms the State Supreme Court's November 28 order directing that Powell be arrested whenever he visits his home state. More than a year later, the court upholds a 30-day sentence assessed against Powell for his contempt of court. The justices sidestep the unresolved puzzle of whether criminal contempt could stem from a civil case.

But then, in April of 1969, the Appellate Division unanimously revises the sentence to 90 days in jail and reduces the finding of criminal contempt to merely civil contempt, sustaining the $250 fine against Powell.

After nine years, the case finally begins to wind down. Everyone embroiled in his legal struggle—everyone except Powell, of course—is exhausted. The suit in Westchester is never resolved; the criminal case in Puerto Rico never gets off the ground; and the suit in Manhattan for the transfer of property in Puerto Rico is never retried.

Rubin and James's epic quest has virtually ground to a halt. The blow dealt them by the Court of Appeals has been devastating. It sets Rubin back well over a year, and the likelihood is small that he will ever win a judgment big enough to justify his expenses and lost time.

The House of Representatives, responding in part to the legal system's inability to collar Powell, has bypassed the courts and kicks Powell off the Hill. Powell then treats his colleagues to a twisted lesson in modern justice: He uses the same court system he defied to prove the House's action illegal. When his case reaches the U. S. Court of Appeals, Warren Burger, writing the court's opinion, avoids the "political question" and refuses to overrule the House. (The House later votes to readmit Powell as a freshman Representative and to fine him $25,000.)

But the U. S. Supreme Court under Chief Justice Earl Warren votes 7-1 in Adam Clayton Powell's favor. The House of Representatives, the justices rule, had improperly excluded Powell from two years of service. The congressman will have to be reseated and could even sue for his unpaid salary for that period.

Afterward, Powell's colleagues rarely see him. He has long since tired of Washington and with his current companion, Darlene Expose, Powell passes the next several years at his Bimini home. There, he relaxes during the election of 1970, in which Charles Rangel narrowly captures his seat in the House—by 250 votes.

And there, in 1972, Adam Clayton Powell, Jr., dies, on the ninth anniversary of his conviction for the defamation of Esther James.

20

Time Troubles: The New Imperative

It is not what a lawyer tells me I may do; but what humanity, reason and justice tell me I ought to do.
—Edmund Burke, "Speech on Conciliation with America," 1775.

By the time *James v. Powell* limped to an end, more than 80 judges sitting in 10 courts had heard parts of the case—many of them several times. The suit was argued in two courts in Puerto Rico; the Manhattan Civil Court; the Appellate Division and the Court of Appeals in New York; Federal District Court; the Federal Circuit Court of Appeals; and the U.S. Supreme Court. Besides the jury in the original defamation trial, three other juries in State Supreme Court heard charges related to this case against Powell as did a grand jury—a total of 59 jurors.

The case attracted the attention of the House of Representatives, the U.S. Attorney General, the New York District Attorney, the F.B.I. (which made a perfunctory investigation of Rubin at Powell's request) and the New York Police Department, which provided protection for James, Rubin and the lawyer's family. The case generated scores of appeals, motions and legal actions against banks, individuals and institutions. All the official papers of the case formed a stack 20 feet high.

While *James v. Powell* concluded years ago, it remains a classic example of how America's legal system is unable to effectively control time in the administration of civil justice—and thus ends up delivering little justice for all. The case shows how the countless ambiguities and complexities built into the law, coupled with skilled legal teams, invite confusion and delay in the courts. It reveals the overuse of our right of appeal; the gross inconsistency of judgments issued from a variety of courts in the same case and usually on the same issue; the inefficiency of our puzzling configuration of court jurisdictions; our abundance of obsolete and counterproductive technical law and finally, the increased use (and overuse) of compromise as a means of ending legal disputes stalled in our crowded courts. Collectively, all of these problems inject huge amounts of time and delays into the judicial process. And it is time, more than anything else, that distorts the system.

Of course, Adam Clayton Powell was no ordinary man. As a prominent black congressman and powerful minister in Harlem, he was able to manipulate a judicial system susceptible to political influence—especially since judges are political appointees. But we must not overstate the peculiar advantage of his public position; it was Powell the man, not the politician, who was able to sidestep the judicial system because of the system's vulnerability to time.

In a broader sense, *James v. Powell* also shows how impotent the law is in forcing action on the part of a person determined to resist legal authority. It can do little to force paying a court-ordered judgment, or even something as simple as showing up in court. The law gives the edge in justice not necessarily to the wealthy but to the defiant: the party who is under legal obligation to comply but refuses to do so. And if the defiant person has no particular vulnerability, such as visible ownership of property or a daily job, he is in an ideal position to evade justice by using time and delay as buffers—until timely justice can no longer be achieved.

Ultimately, however, we don't need to design a new legal system; we need a *new imperative*. We must focus on ways to speed up the current system, wringing out time-killing processes and delay tactics that do not advance just outcomes. The notion that more time produces better justice is an antiquated abstraction. In reality, it supports another legal precedent: the law of diminishing returns.

As I noted earlier, the biggest time fix requires a broad physical expansion of the judicial structure itself, including the small claims court system. In order to handle many more cases within a reasonable, predictable time frame, we need to enlarge its administrative structure—perhaps as much as 10 times. Granted, such an expensive expansion needs to be phased in over a span of years, but *it must be done*. Our court system is just as important a part of our nation's infrastructure as our roads and bridges and our educational system.

Our volume of civil cases has grown exponentially over the last century, and yet we have done little to improve a judicial system that was designed largely to resolve legal disputes in an agrarian society. Our courts must be reengineered to meet the needs of citizens working and living in a complex, high-tech, high-speed era where financial, commercial and emotional issues of litigation demand speed. Our new imperative requires that cases be brought into the court system within six months, not burdened with pretrial papers and procedures that add little but time, money and frustration.

Just imagine:

If the new high school opened in your community, and instead of the expected 2,000 students, the enrollment mushroomed to 2,700. Would you handle the increased volume by simply saying, "Oh well, I guess the kids will have to finish high school in eight years instead of four"?

Of course not!

You'd find ways to hire more teachers, create more classes and, if necessary, increase the size of the facility so that all students have the opportunity to finish within the prescribed time. Why does our school system get so much more support than our legal system? Because its constituency—the PTAs, the teachers' unions, the local civic associations—is much better organized. The citizens who litigate have no organized effort as a group. They are without lobbyists or friends in government; they need to take the system as they find it and try to make it work.

Nevertheless, we must come together somehow as a collective voice and forge the political will to address this judicial infrastructure crisis. The court system must be able to provide procedures that are fast enough to reinforce good behavior by participants—rather than allowing demoralizing delays that sanction bad behavior.

As I've pointed out earlier, a number of small, specific time fixes can greatly help speed the judicial process, such as broadening the roles of magistrates and the authority of judges; modifying service notification; settling jurisdictional disputes up front; codifying monetary awards; and barring most contingency fee arrangements.

Furthermore, we must relieve lawyers from the obligatory task of preparing lengthy briefs that take days to write and hours to read—and respond to—and allow them to argue their clients' needs orally before a judge in court. Why do we think justice must be the written word? If our legal system placed a premium on oral argument rather than the written word, lay people would find the courts a more hospitable forum in which to seek justice on their own. Today, depositions have become complete and comprehensive tools used to gather information; what that does is *rehearse* everybody, taking away the freshness of the case, the spontaneity. The question is, why would we want the judge and jury to see anything other than the first-time testimony, instead of the cynical experience that comes from telling the story repeatedly over time? Let the people tell their stories. And let the judges decide what's legally right and wrong. They know the law.

Certainly, we don't need to do away with all written briefs and motions, but we can reduce them drastically and dramatically. Keep them short; use them as a secondary alternative to verbal argument and make them work to speed the system along. When we allow trials like *James v. Powell* to take thousands of pages of testimony to complete, we violate our society's need for swift, accessible justice.

Even in the area of legal contracts, the most effective approach to timely enforcement may have been demonstrated by my client Freeman McNeil, the former New York Jets player, who put his trust in an oral agreement with team owners, rather than a written contract. It was a highly unusual move, given a growing culture of contentious posturing and negotiating tactics in professional sports.

McNeil was a formidable running back, an All-Pro player drafted in the first round out of UCLA. But he was a very gentle man, a noble, principled and sensitive person toiling in a violent sport.

In the twilight of his career during the early 1990s, McNeil requested that management give him a final two-year agreement so he could complete an 11-year stint in the National Football League with the Jets. He requested a no-trade provision as part of the contract. During the negotiations, the issues of salary, bonuses and other provisions were resolved, but one irreconcilable point remained—the request for a no-trade provision. Steve Guttman, the Jets president at the time, objected to this provision, asserting that the no-trade limitation took away the prerogatives of management and thus was inconsistent with club policy. The Jets would not trade McNeil, Guttman said, but he would not put the promise in writing. McNeil trusted Guttman and Leon Hess, the principal owner of the Jets, and he accepted their oral promise not to trade him. The contract was signed without the no-trade clause.

At a time when everybody insists, "Put it in writing," can we—or should we—trust an oral promise? McNeil and the Jets seemed to have stepped back in time to a period when "a man's word was his bond." Perhaps they simply understood that the real basis of timely enforceability was trust, relying on the promises of the right *people,* rather than on the written document.

Many who experience the legal system corroded by time have lost respect not just for the courts, but for all legality. They recognize the system's vulnerability and wonder whether contracts should be obeyed; thus, the imperative for compliance is critically weakened. Legal agreements of all sorts are casually discarded when living within their provisions becomes inconvenient—and unenforceable in any timely manner.

From my years of experience in championship yacht racing, I learned the importance of having grievance processes that move quickly to resolve issues. If you make a mistake, you can take the penalty or you can protest it. Before you start the race the next day, the matter's done; everybody knows where he stands in the race and you move forward. Even if you feel the decision is not entirely fair, if it's quick, at least it's humane.

Of course, when deciding complex legal issues that could shape the fate of society, we should continue to allow cases to climb deliberately through the Appellate Court system. But let the cases of commerce—monetary and property rights—be decided in a system more like the marketplace in which these disputes arose: with quick and businesslike resolutions. All litigation is painful, but the pain is magnified by the enormous financial and emotional difficulties of lengthy lawsuits on individuals, their families and the organizations they work for. It's time to balance the exhaustive procedures of due process with the right to obtain timely justice. In the end, a system's pursuit of perfection, if not balanced by practical needs, fails.

More than 40 years ago, Supreme Court Chief Justice Warren Burger made this ominous observation in an address to the American Bar Association: One of several societal changes that could destroy confidence in the courts was "that people come to believe that inefficiency and delay will drain even a just judgment of its value."

The risk of the breakdown in our legal system is no less profound than that of a breakdown in the economic system. The courts provide our cultural building blocks; they teach our citizens the rules of a society—our *common morality*, as reflected in the law. The legal system works only so long as most Americans believe that the legality taught by the courts coincides with their own ideas of morality.

But in contemporary society, we have witnessed a decline in religious and moral teachings, coupled with the lack of confidence in the legal system, that has led people to establish their own sets of values, idiosyncratic social relationships and perceptions of right and wrong. Moral values are no longer common but transactional in nature, and, in many respects, convenient. That is why we see so many individualistic lifestyles, so much peculiar and self-dealing behavior that doesn't seem grounded in any sort of principle except self-preservation and self-advancement.

In a free society, the most solemn obligation a government assumes is the responsibility to provide a legal system that, when disputes arise, guarantees each citizen prompt and even application of the law. This obligation forms the vital covenant between the government and its citizens, for they pledge their patriotism to the nation only in return for this guaranteed right. As 18th century philosopher Jean-Jacques Rousseau stated in his seminal work, *The Social Contract*, the basis of a social system is a fundamental pact that "substitutes a moral and lawful equality for the physical inequality which nature imposed upon men, so that...they all become equal by convention and legal right."

While the legal maxim "Justice delayed is justice denied" is attributed to the great 19th century British politician, William Gladstone, its origins go much deeper into the foundations of Western democracy. Indeed, the phrase may be traced to a clause of the Magna Carta of 1215, which reads, "to no one will we refuse or delay, right or justice." And in 17th century America, William Penn, the founder of Pennsylvania, included a similar aphorism in his pithy volume, *Some Fruits of Solitude*: "To delay justice, is injustice."

Over the years, the American legal system has evolved according to the will of its people, ensuring continuous "moral and lawful equality." But the administration of the law has not evolved fast enough to match the needs of a culture driven by accelerating technological change.

Time, indeed, is of the essence.

Before some dreadful hour, we must reestablish its

base of support for our legal system and make it reflect the good in its people instead of their defiance. Through our mastery of time, the judicial system will derive great strength and we shall assure future generations of Americans of their freedom.

Appendix:
The Short List of Time Fixes

Substantially reduce pretrial paperwork

Modify service notification procedures

Broadly expand the court system

Require plaintiffs to pay all expenses if appeal is lost

Bar percentage contingency fees

Enforce court decisions

Require litigants to attend all court proceedings

Expand small claims court

Settle jurisdictional disputes up front

Codify monetary awards

Keep the same judges on a case

Expand the role of magistrates

Broaden authority of judges

Set trial date after answer is served

Acknowledgments

Over many years, there have been a number of people who have been important to me as a person and as a lawyer. I want to take this opportunity to thank them publicly. Thank you, Harrison Salisbury. Thanks to all my law partners, in particular, Barbara Alesi, Tony Barton and Jeff Forchelli. For their guidance and inspiration, thanks to Father Tom Hartman and Harry Chapin. Thanks to my oldest and dearest friend, Hon. John G. DiNoto. My sincere appreciation goes to those whom I've worked for and with—Alan Jusko, Robert Eckhardt, Ron Greenstone, Chester Broman and Ed Salzano. Jim Lamarca and Jeff Barasch—you have my sincere appreciation. And finally, for the many hours of stimulating discussions, relaxation and fun, I want to thank my friends Pascal Perri, Don Condit, Glen Maaser and the "Big Guy," Danny Martin.

All of you, individually and collectively, have truly enriched my life.